W9-BZX-755

# EARLY CHILDHOOD EDUCATION SERIES

**Leslie R. Williams, Editor**
**Millie Almy, Senior Advisor**

ADVISORY BOARD: **Barbara T. Bowman, Harriet K. Cuffaro, Stephanie Feeney, Doris Pronin Fromberg, Celia Genishi, Dominic F. Gullo, Alice Sterling Honig, Elizabeth Jones, Gwen Morgan, David Weikart**

# THE
# GOOD PRESCHOOL
# TEACHER

## Six Teachers Reflect on Their Lives

## WILLIAM AYERS

Foreword by Vivian Gussin Paley

Teachers College, Columbia University
New York and London

Published by Teachers College Press, 1234 Amsterdam Avenue,
New York, NY 10027

Library of Congress Cataloging-in-Publication Data

Ayers, William, 1944–
    The good preschool teacher.

    (Early childhood education series)
    Bibliography: p. 153
    Includes index.
    1. Preschool teaching—United States.   2. Preschool
teachers—United States.   1. Title.   II. Series.
LB1775.5.A97   1989      372'.21      88-29641

ISBN 0-8077-2947-7
ISBN 0-8077-2946-9 (pbk.)

Manufactured in the United States of America

99  98  97  96  95       4  5  6  7  8

# CONTENTS

# FOREWORD

There should be a sign above every classroom door that reads, "All teachers who enter: Be prepared to tell your story."

We teachers are more curious about the children than about ourselves. Our every action reveals the shadow of our urgent preoccupation, but seldom is there anyone around to question the questioner.

A child's images are fairly accessible, for children cannot help but act them out in monologue and play. We, however, performing in more covert ways, are less likely to have our themes analyzed and recorded.

The six teachers described here are fortunate. Having learned to listen carefully to the children, it is now their turn to be heard. They have been given the best gift of all: a good listener who knows the territory. William Ayers brings to his interviews a broad understanding of children and society, and he shapes for us a distinct context within which to study each teacher's responses.

Ayers does not leave himself out of the picture. His story too must be known if we are to identify the choices he makes as he sets the stage and interprets the action. In this process of self-examination and reflection, no one is excluded.

But where does a teacher's story begin? In college, we studied "faceless" children and were given maps that promised to tell us where every child lives. Yet we felt anonymous and were unable to locate ourselves on the maps.

How could we expect otherwise? We may learn the language and customs of our profession elsewhere, but life in the classroom is lived primarily in the classroom—for that matter, in all the classrooms and around all the kitchen tables we have known. Every time we greet a new child, the script must be rewritten.

The preschool teachers in this book can indeed be called "good." They know how to talk to children and show them affection. Their dialogues are warm, personal, and open-ended; each child receives the teacher's attention and respect in seemingly endless quantity.

Why then do teachers who already are this good need to explain what they do? For what purpose must they resurrect memory and motive? It is because love and intuition are not enough, and neither are books and lectures. If teachers are to continue to grow they must at some point begin to study themselves. They must one day ask their own questions, such as: What really is going on here? What do my words mean? What am I missing?

Children have ways of studying themselves. They use fantasy play—that most primitive form of storytelling—to uncover areas of doubt and hold them up to public view. The result often is a great surge of energy that leads to further discoveries.

We too must find the means by which to explore our inner monologues and rekindle the original life force children so readily express. In re-examining our background and biases we open the possibility for making new connections between our behavior and the children's. We may begin to see more clearly the vast differences in children as they try to fit themselves into the mold of our expectations.

What a shame we can't all be interviewed by William Ayers, who has the rare ability to teach as he questions. However, he gives us clear and strong examples of how the process can work. Perhaps, somewhere in these six biographies, our own questions will begin to emerge.

VIVIAN GUSSIN PALEY
UNIVERSITY OF CHICAGO
LABORATORY SCHOOLS

# PREFACE

This book is the result of a sustained inquiry into the work and lives of preschool teachers. The point of the study is to examine in detail the work of a few teachers, to construct with each a meaningful account of her life, and to consider how her own self-understanding has had an impact on her teaching practice.

One assumption of this inquiry is that teachers are a rich and worthy source of knowledge about teaching. The "secret" of teaching is in the detail of everyday practice, and it is to individual teachers that we must turn in order to best understand teaching. A second assumption is that since teachers are the chief instruments of their own practice—teaching is not a fixed curriculum or method applicable to all situations—teacher self-awareness is valuable, perhaps indispensable. Teachers are always, in the last analysis, thrust back upon themselves as the inventors of their own efforts and the authors of their own teaching texts. A third assumption of this study is that teachers are interactive professionals, "reflective practitioners" to use Donald Schön's (1983) term, who draw on training, skill, a growing body of experience, habit, personal values, art, science, and native wit to do their work. Teachers are not scientists (at least not in their teaching roles) because they are not engaged in an activity that is fundamentally technical or objective. Teachers are necessarily idiosyncratic and improvisational, sometimes relying on science, as architects at times must do, and often applying accumulated experiential knowledge in transcendent ways, as midwives do. Teachers are always engaged in reflective conversations with endlessly unique situations.

The heart of this book is six portraits of preschool teachers teaching and reflecting on their pathways to the present moment. The teachers of this study are Anna Tiant, a woman who works with infants and toddlers; Chana Stein, a family home day-care provider; JoAnne Williams, a teacher at a collectively run day-care center; Michele Wilson, a pre-kindergarten teacher in a public school; Darlene Mosley, a teacher of young children at a unique program for homeless children; and Maya Dawson, a kindergarten teacher in a progressive private school. Each of these names is fictitious in order to protect the privacy of the teachers. All six are outstanding and experienced teachers, having logged many years in preschool. My three-dimensional portraits of these teachers are intended to show a range of what is possible in preschools, not what is common or what is likely. They are intended to provide practical examples of excellence in the field, to motivate those starting out, and to inspire and perhaps instruct those more experienced in early childhood education. They are also meant to inform parents and others who are struggling to understand this explosively growing and yet largely undefined field.

There are very little hard, unambiguous data on the need and availability of child care in this country. We know that over half of the more than eight million mothers with children under six are in the labor force, and we know that there are more than nine million children with working mothers. We know that families are changing, that more and more families are headed by women, and that more and more mothers work outside the home. And we know that adequate, affordable child care is difficult to find and hard to arrange. But we don't know much about what programs exist and about what characterizes those programs. These portraits can help focus our discussion of quality in child care and ground our debates about policy in the real world of children, families, and teachers.

Finally, this book develops a method of autobiographical reflection that may be useful in preservice teacher education or in-service teacher renewal efforts. This method, which requires no equipment or expensive consultants and outside experts, is accessible to anyone with the time to develop a series of reflective activities and the interest to work both collaboratively and independently. It is my hope that this method will prove effective to those involved in the improvement of teaching.

# ACKNOWLEDGMENTS

Thanks are due to Laurie Schreiber, Janice Molnar, Sharon Coleman, and Sharon Steffensen for hard work, patience, and invaluable assistance. My appreciation goes to editors Susan Liddicoat, Myra Cleary, and Nina George, for their helpful revisions of the text.

My deepest gratitude to Leslie Williams and Karen Zumwalt for reading and re-reading, supporting, and pushing.

Thanks to Ray McDermott for challenging and nurturing.

Special thanks to Maxine Greene, mentor, colleague, inspiration, and friend.

Thank you to all those who taught me about teaching: Jane Alexander, Nancy Balaban, Cleo Banks, Nancy Barrett, Dorothy Bloomfield, Frances Bolin, Eleanor Brussel, Happie Byers, Michael Cook, Lyn Corno, Harriet Cuffaro, George Dennison, Amy Dombro, Hubert Dyasi, Janet Fraidstern, Joe Grannis, Lin Goodwin, Toby Hendon, Barbara Hernandez, Arthur Hochman, John Holt, Heidi Jacobs, Bruce Kanze, Herb Kohl, Pat Lee, Ann Lieberman, Judy Leipzig, Leah Levinger, Debby Meier, Jan Miller, Judi Minter, Elaine Myrianthopoulos, Katie O'Donnell, Beth Oglesby, Ned O'Gorman, Diana Oughton, Harry Passow, Vito Perrone, Denise Prince, B. J. Richards, José Rivera, Kathy Roberts, Frances Rust, Toni Savage, Yvonne Smith, Kate Sullivan, Skip Taube, Rachel Theilheimer, Gus Trowbridge, Hervé Varenne, José Vega, Rachel Walpole, Lillian Weber, Miriam Westheimer, and more.

A kiss to my Mom and Dad for their early teaching, their care, and their generous support.

A bear hug to my most persistent teachers: Zayd, Malik, and Chesa.

To Bernardine Dohrn, who taught me to value the valuable and to stay wide awake to the possible—thank you again.

Finally, heartfelt thanks for their time, care, and dedication to this project go to the six outstanding teachers who continue to inspire through their teaching.

Multiple small spheres of personal experience both echo and enable events shared more widely, expressions of moment in which we recognize that no microcosm is completely separate, no tide pool, no forest, no family, no nation. Indeed, the knowledge drawn from the life of some single organism or community or from the intimate experience of an individual may prove to be relevant to decisions that affect the health of a city or the peace of the world.

MARY CATHERINE BATESON

# THE
# GOOD PRESCHOOL
# TEACHER

# ★ 1 ★

# SAYING LIVES
## Being and Teaching

The main purpose of this book is to hear the voices of six teachers and to render their stories. Accordingly, the method I used is necessarily qualitative and naturalistic, an attempt to capture descriptive accounts of teachers teaching as well as telling stories of teaching and of becoming teachers. As we shall see, these aspects are united in the creation of individual portraits of teachers working and reflecting upon their own actions. The goal is to expand our understanding of the meaning teachers give to their work, to perceive in the particular details of these portraits patterns that will perhaps prove useful to them as well as relevant to others, and to move toward the development of a method of teacher self-awareness and self-reporting.

Of course, this work occurs in a context and at a particular moment in educational history, a moment when Americans are once again talking about reforming the schools. In the past four or five years there has been a virtual blizzard of reports from local, state, and national commissions on education, accompanied by a flood of popular newspaper and magazine articles, television special reports, and running commentary from politicians and policy makers. Education is once again the focus of intense hope and heated criticism. From the point of view of educators, all this attention and focus can be encouraging, hopeful, and heady stuff: Discussion is now legitimized, new ideas are placed on the agenda, and, most important, the educational enterprise appears to approach center stage, where many of us think it belongs. Teachers are encouraged when they see the nation caring about the issues in which they have invested their lives, and teachers are energized when they hear people in high places commenting on their most intimate and abiding concerns.

But not all of the attention is wonderful. Optimism is tempered by the direction and content of much of the discussion, and hope is suspended by the messages conveyed by some of the powerful voices. Prescriptions for the schools are too often of the quick-fix variety and come in the form of proclamations from above with little appreciation for the contexts and needs of particular children in particular classrooms. Neither do they address the real-life concerns of specific families and teachers. When

1

this happens, the policy-making, managerial perspective overwhelms the messy, idiosyncratic nature of children and teachers in schools, and the truth of nuance and subtlety is lost in the interest of smooth and formal problem solving. There appears to be no understanding in much of the reform debate, for example, about the importance of the powerful school ethos and the classroom culture, crucial elements in any meaningful discussion of educational reform.

Too often reform proposals are based on narrow models of education, models that ignore the importance of emotions, values, intentions, and attitudes, models that promote a limited notion of academics as the primary thread of what constitutes intellectual engagement and growth. If education, for example, is conceived simply as a method designed to reproduce existing social relations, then education for self-discovery and self-determination is lost, and any thought of empowering the young to transcend the present and invent their own futures is forfeited. Particularly tragic in this regard is that so much of the present discussion is premised on attacking the modest gains made in the past 30 years in the nation's commitment to educating black children as well as other children of color, either by ignoring the special responsibilities that correspond to that commitment or by insistently repeating, in the context of a massive retreat from support for urban public education, the fact that schools cannot solve every social problem.

The context of my inquiry, then, necessarily includes this particular moment we are experiencing in educational history. A remarkable feature of this season of school reform is seen when we identify the missing voices. Teachers, working at the very heart of the educational enterprise, are among the silent. Where in the national reports are the voices of teachers? Where are the voices of families and children—voices of engagement, responsibility, investment, involvement, and firsthand knowledge? Where are the living accounts of those most intimately bound up with schools?

Because they are invisible in their own worlds, teachers (along with children and parents) are dehumanized, de-intellectualized, and disempowered by many of the current reports on education. Studies continue this offense when they deny teachers voice and context. On the other hand, teachers are humanized when their lived lives, their real and varied experiences, and their unique situations and pathways to teaching are accounted for. Teachers are dignified when they are assumed to be a rich and powerful source of knowledge about teaching, when they are looked upon as people who are essential in making some sense out of the intricate and complex phenomena that they know best. And, most important, meaningful school improvement, improvement that really touches the lives of teachers and children in schools, is necessarily a process that takes hold on the inside and therefore depends on an understanding of the subjective world of the classroom.

Recently some effort has been made to listen to the teacher's voice, but interestingly, little of this work has focused on the lives of preschool teachers. Preschool teachers appear to be seen either as glorified baby-sitters whose working lives are unrelated to the lives of other teachers, or as a subset of teachers generally, without exceptional and important characteristics of their own. In the former view, they are outside the circle of education, outside the profession of teaching, and unworthy of serious attention. In the latter view, they are an appendage of teaching generally, the poor cousins within the profession as a whole. In either case the voices of preschool teachers are even less heeded than those of teachers generally.

This is sad. Not only is the work of preschool teachers devalued in this way, but a potentially powerful voice for all children is brushed aside in the process. For preschool teachers have developed common practices that make sense at all levels—practices like including children's own knowledge and experience as a basis for curriculum development, accepting a broad range of behavior as "normal," and responding to children as whole people with complex, interconnected intentions and needs. Unfortunately the tenor and tone of the current educational discussion almost universally assume a "trickle-down" effect in which the needs of international competition, the economy, and the military dictate to the colleges and high schools, and the demand for a reconstituted curriculum trickles down to middle and elementary school. Kindergarten and preschool reconstruction become linked to the "reformed" elementary school, and so it goes. In the process, preschool teachers are left speechless. Perhaps a healthier, stronger, and more productive direction of reform would be to allow reform to "trickle up." In this way some of the taken-for-granted practices in preschool might begin to inform all education. Several observers have noted that the simple facts of life in kindergarten—the need for fairness, for example, to put things back where they were, and to clean up messes made—are a sensible starting point in addressing the overarching social problems of our time.

## RATIONALE

In the early 1980s I studied three teachers at work as part of an ethnographic inquiry of early childhood education. Maya was a teacher in a progressive private school kindergarten, Anna worked in an infant-toddler center, and JoAnne ran her own day-care program. Several years later I worked on a study of teaching and autobiography with Michele, a public school prekindergarten teacher; Chana, a group family day-care provider; and again JoAnne. Still later I observed and interviewed Darlene because I was drawn to the uniqueness of her powerful project of providing day care to the children of homeless families.

As I constructed this book, I brought these different portraits together under one roof. Like the rooms of a house, some are big and some small, some elaborate and some simple. Several of the differences in quality and focus are attributable to the different contexts out of which each portrait emerged. And some of the unevenness, in terms of depth of analysis or richness of synthesis, is similarly the result of the distinct purposes each portrait served at the time it was developed. For me each portrait tells an important story of a teacher's life, and each story can extend our sense of the value of early childhood education.

Many people have asked why this project deals exclusively with women teachers. My answer is simple: Preschool teaching is almost entirely a woman's world. When one looks for examples of outstanding practice in a field that is 98 percent female, one quite naturally encounters women. There are of course some fine men working with young children (I tried for quite awhile, in fact, to gain access to a hospital-based day-care center for children with AIDS, where an outstanding young man worked, but was continually rebuffed by the administration). The best of the male preschool teachers tend to acknowledge the appropriateness of women attaining recognition and providing leadership in a field that is overwhelmingly of their making.

Clearly I chose in this work to discover a lot about a few teachers, rather than a little about a lot of teachers. Instead of aggregating teachers in a search for the common teacher, the point here was to celebrate the particular, the uncommon, and the unpredictable. This choice was based on a strong belief that it is in the lived situations of actual teachers—rather than in, for example, the educational commissions, policy panels, or research institutions—that the teaching enterprise exists and can best be understood. This required seeing the reality of teaching and teachers in as full a context as possible. The "secret" of teaching after all is in the detail of everyday practice, the very stuff that is washed away in attempts to generalize about teaching. The goal here was not to predict, but perhaps to extend our sense of the possible by portraying some of the breadth and scope of what preschool teaching can be. We do not, of course, end up with the truth, but perhaps more modestly with a burgeoning sense of meaning and knowing grounded in real people and concrete practices.

Since reform proposals, curriculum units, and administrative directives ultimately live or die in the hands of individual teachers, it is to individual teachers that we ultimately turn in order to understand teaching. It is true of course that no teacher is an island, or a perfectly free agent. Teachers, in common with the rest of us, are shaped by powerful social and economic forces, which coerce and constrain, prod and bombard, push and pull. Teachers particularly are formed by their relationships to power and their role in a bureaucracy geared to reproducing the societal relations in general.

But it is also true that teachers finally decide what goes on in classrooms. When the door is closed and the noise from outside and inside has settled, a teacher chooses. She can decide to satisfy distant demands or not, accommodate established expectations or not, embrace her narrowest self-interest or not. She can decide whether to merely survive another day of inexhaustible demands and limited energy, or she can decide, for example, to interpret and invent, and resist and rebel where necessary. She can decide to link up with others in order to create something different. There are all kinds of ways to choose, and we will see in these pages accounts of people acting out of varying degrees and senses of self-awareness and deliberation, people inventing their teaching in a world that is often resistant and always problematic.

I was interested in seeing teachers at work, but also in understanding how they came to be the teachers they are. I felt that by observing them and then asking them to help me better understand some of the details of their work—both phenomenologically and from the perspective of historical precedent—we would be able to construct a life-narrative that would be an honest attempt at self-awareness. This kind of exercise, I thought, had the potential to become a powerful tool in teacher education as well as teacher renewal. In becoming more self-conscious, I figured, teachers could also become more intentional, more able to endorse or reject aspects of their own teaching that they found hopeful or contrary, more able to author their own teaching scripts.

Although we note that powerful forces in society have serious and intricate designs on schools, we also acknowledge that any designs must finally be filtered through the minds and the hearts and the hands of teachers. And while teachers may be cajoled or fooled, or (as in these times) threatened or punished, into accepting and implementing certain practices, they also might not be. In looking at teachers we are looking at the base of the educational pyramid (and in looking at preschool teachers we are at the lower end of the bottom). Ironically, if we look closely enough, we are also looking at the peak of power and possibility.

## METHOD

In developing the teacher portraits presented in this book, I used a method of inquiry involving two interconnected yet overlapping phases. In the first phase, I conducted intense and extensive observations in each of the six preschool settings. From my detailed field notes, I wrote ethnographic accounts that depicted six teachers teaching. I will say more about ethnography in the next section. In the second phase, a variety of techniques were used to encourage those teachers to reflect on their lives as they affect their teaching practice. Information gathered from these two phases was studied and analyzed in a search for meaningful patterns, and in the end I created portraits of teachers teaching and reflecting on the meaning of their life stories as those stories influenced their teaching. These portraits—the result of observing teachers, constructing ethnographic accounts of their teaching, listening to them talk about why they teach as they do and how they came to be the teachers they are, and creating a life-narrative with each—are intended as a contribution to the available natural history of teaching. The purpose here is to discover how these teachers understand themselves and how they locate themselves on their own particular pedagogical journeys.

During the observation phase of the study, I functioned essentially as a participant-observer in each classroom over several days. While I was collecting detailed notes, mapping spaces, diagramming, and describing each teacher in the context of a specific setting, I was also (as any visitor to a preschool setting will identify with) reading to groups of children, wiping noses, changing diapers, and zipping up coats. Information was analyzed continuously in an attempt to move from broad to more focused and selected accounts of practice, to uncover new questions, and to reckon with patterns as they emerged. The observations were guided by my own intuition and experience, and focused on the structures and routines of each setting, the interactions among the children as well as between the adults and the children, the actions of the teacher, the explicit and implicit goals of each program, and the feeling or tone of each group.

Interviews were a part of the second phase and tended to be informal, allowing for a more equal footing between the teacher and me than is possible in many traditional research settings. My goal was to create an open-ended, negotiable situation. Besides interviews, this study utilized written correspondence between the teachers and me. Based sometimes on classroom observations and sometimes on more general questions, I sent notes to each teacher asking questions of general interest or about particular observed events. The notes included open requests like, "Describe a particularly successful moment in your work last week," and specific ones like, "Describe why you responded as you did to the difficult separation between Amy and her mother yesterday." The teacher's response was in the form of a vignette, a brief word sketch. The dialogue had immediacy as well as development over time. Furthermore, the notes probed for antecedents, for historical knowledge, for autobiographical explanation. The notes sought context and description, reflection and conclusion, current insight and historical precedent.

The most interesting area of inquiry, which is less traditional than either interviews or vignettes, employed in this second phase, was the use of "non-linear" or "interpretive" activities (Bolin, 1986). An example of a non-linear activity that many people engage in spontaneously is doodling. Focused interpretive activities explore the same ground as interviews or vignettes but without the heavy reliance on speaking or writing. They involve working with familiar materials (paper, clay, and paint, for example) to represent or symbolize salient experiences. Interpretive activities disengage people from conscious thought and can provide fresh insight and significant discoveries.

For example, an interpretive activity that I used here involved teachers working with clay to depict particularly successful moments in teaching. This is not unlike being asked in an interview to describe a successful moment in teaching, but it offers the possibility of responding to this question in new and surprising ways.

These kinds of activities were tools to round out the store of information about how these teachers see themselves and their work, and to uncover the images these teachers hold about teaching. There was an emphasis on feelings and attitudes, emotions and values. Each activity led to sharing through discussion, but the conversation was animated by the concrete action, the play at hand. Dimensions not easily apprehended in interviews—like affective dimensions, and spiritual and cultural dimensions—were more naturally addressed here.

Often this disengagement in play proved to be an easier, lighter way to discover relevant moments and led to new insights and deeper, more significant discoveries. It proved on many occasions to be a rich experience, suspending the kind of "reconstructed logic" (Kaplan, 1963) that so often dominates historical accounts. As William Pinar (1975) noted about free association, the degree to which one can "fall into past experience" and "relive early and present experiences" is the degree to which information is "phenomenologically accurate" (p. 408). Non-linear, interpretive activities helped ground this project in phenomenological accuracy.

In interviews, vignettes, and interpretive activities, the goal was to produce a meaningful narrative text that described and linked together influences, events, people, and experiences that contributed to the creation of the teacher as she finds herself today. Probing the significance of current activity and reconstructing a meaningful past created the conditions for each teacher, speaking in her own voice, to critically examine teaching practices and locate them in a continuum from past to future. What emerged was a kind of autobiography, although the word "autobiography" seemed too heavy, too loaded with earth-shaking expectations for the participants. My word was "co-biography" in an attempt to highlight the centrality of collaboration in this project, but that word seemed awkward and unreal too, and so was rarely used. "Life-narratives" was the handy and unanimous usage for what we were constructing, and it was the life-narratives combined with the ethnographic accounts that emerged as the portraits of preschool teachers. As I developed each portrait I gave a copy to the teacher for revision, comment, and criticism. As far as possible I have retained the original sketch and allowed the response and ensuing dialogue to become another layer enriching the emerging portrait of that teacher.

With the telling of each story, these teachers became more consciously writers of their own scripts and readers of their own lives. This process led to an awareness of aspects of their own practices that had been obscure or unavailable to them before. This awakening to previously unknown worlds, this seeing anew, gave them and may give other teachers in other places and times clearer access to choice, greater freedom to become the teachers they want to be—more active and vital participants in their own reflective practice.

The kinds of information that contributed to my undertaking ranged widely (Beginnings, 1986; Feiman-Nemser & Floden, 1984; Lightfoot, 1973; Lortie, 1975; Schön, 1983; Smyth, 1984.) The questions covered are easily transferable for use by others engaging in similar inquiry projects, and can be grouped for convenience into three broad areas of concern.

## 1. The Reflective Practitioner

- What do you like most about teaching? What are the rewards for you? When do you feel best as a teacher? What are your favorite moments?
- What is most difficult about teaching? Do you ever feel like leaving the profession? Why? Why do you stay? If you could, what things would you change in your work?
- Which children appeal to you? Why? Which ones make your work problematic?
- What is the role of parents in your work? What should it be?

- Why is your space arranged the way it is? Why do you follow particular routines?
- Why do you teach as you do? What criteria do you have in mind? What do you take to be valuable in your teaching? What other teachers do you admire? Why?
- What is your role in the lives of children and families? What are your goals for children? How do you meet these goals?
- What is your role in preparing children for the future? Are there any conflicts between your goals and the school's goals? Society's goals? If so, do the conflicts affect the children?

### 2. The Autobiographer

- Can you describe any chance factors that led to your becoming a teacher? Are you sometimes surprised to see what you have become?
- When did you decide to become a teacher? What did your decision mean to you at that time? What was it about teaching that interested or attracted you?
- What role, explicitly or implicitly, did your family play in your decision to teach? Do you remember any early experiences that affected your decision to teach?
- Do you remember any outstanding teachers from your years as a student? What do you remember? Did this influence your decision in any way?
- What was your formal teacher education like? Did it prepare you for the realities of teaching? Is teaching pretty much what you'd expected? When you first taught were there any colleagues or mentors who influenced you? How?
- Can you remember when you felt comfortable as a teacher, confident with your own philosophy and practical knowledge?
- Can you think of early experiences that continue to influence what and how you teach now? Can you describe the central teaching ideas that guide your work, and how you came to adopt them?
- Have you changed as a teacher over the years? How?

### 3. The Whole Person

- What is of value to you beyond teaching? Are you involved in any social or political groups?
- What concerns you most about children and families today? About the state of society or the world?

- Are you involved in any other projects or interests outside of teaching? What? How are they important to you?
- What have you read recently that was significant to you?
- What do you imagine you'll be doing in five years? In ten years?

Like others who have studied teachers, I was looking at an enterprise that is complex, idiosyncratic, and largely mysterious, something David Denton (1974) describes as a "world of intentional action, individuated and shared meanings, affectional ties, tensive relationships, in which there is always the possibility of one's saying no" (p. 108). I was looking at people who are assumed to be moral, self-determining agents even as they are entangled and constrained by a host of pressures and factors. And I was looking at six lives—not categories or summaries—being lived in a shared world. I was attempting to hear their voices, to attend to their stories with care and hope. Underneath it all, this project was shaped by a vision best expressed by Maxine Greene (1978):

> Persons are more likely to ask their own questions and seek their own tran-
> scendence when they feel themselves grounded in their personal histories,
> their lived lives. That is what I mean by "landscapes." A human being lives,
> as it were, in two orders—one created by his or her relations with the
> perceptual fields that are given in experience, the other created by his or
> her relations with a human and social environment. It is important to hold
> in mind, therefore, that each of us achieved contact with the world from a
> particular vantage point, in terms of a particular biography. All of this un-
> derlies our present perspective and affects the way we look at things and
> talk about things and structure our realities. To be in touch with our land-
> scapes is to be conscious of our evolving experiences, to be aware of the
> ways in which we encounter our world. (p. 2)

## QUALITATIVE INQUIRY

I want to go into a bit more detail about the thinking behind the method of this work. I begin with a discussion of ethnography generally and then move to a more specific discussion of the value of autobiography in educational studies and the concrete use of portraiture in this project.

### Ethnography

Ethnography is a term initially used by cultural anthropologists to describe both their attempts to discover and discern different cultures, as

well as the written accounts produced as a result of fieldwork conducted in those various cultures. Ethnography embraces this dual sense—the study-in-process and the product-of-study. One can be said to be "doing ethnography," that is, conducting an ethnographic inquiry in the field, or "writing an ethnography," that is, working up a report based upon that inquiry.

"Doing ethnography" consists of "gathering fieldnotes in a context of fieldwork" (Wolcott, n.d.). Clifford Geertz (1973) offers a textbook definition of "doing ethnography" as "establishing rapport, selecting informants, transcribing texts, taking genealogies, mapping fields, keeping a diary, and so on" (p. 6). Producing an ethnography, on the other hand, is the result of rigorous analysis and paying riveted attention to field notes. "Being there" (Geertz, 1988) and then portraying a different life in the context of a specific culture—conveying the insider's sense-making view—is the essence of ethnography.

Ethnography is clearly a more elusive concept than, say, "process-product research," and understandably it describes an activity that is less likely to be apprehended in a straightforward way. There is no simple mechanism of ethnography, no ready recipe of ethnographic inquiry, no methodological machine that, once started, runs itself. Rather, ethnography is as dynamic and complex as the human beings it undertakes to study. Hervé Varenne (1986) argues that "ethnographic research is a human activity . . . generated, made possible, constrained and helped by the same conditions which generate, make possible, constrain and help all activities" (p. 1).

Obviously there is not a single definition of ethnographic research that is wholly illuminating or fully satisfactory, just as there is no model ethnographic account that can stand as an embracing example of ethnographic reports. There is, however, an ethnographic sensibility, a body of work, and a respectable tradition upon which to draw and with which to interact. Again, Clifford Geertz (1973) notes that what defines ethnography is "the kind of intellectual effort it is: an elaborate venture in, to borrow a notion from Gilbert Ryle, thick description" (p. 6).

In a sense, ethnography is to other, more traditional and strongly warranted social science inquiry, what jazz is to music (Agar, 1980). That is, ethnography is unquestionably intuitive, idiosyncratic, and improvisational. These features, however, far from making it an illegitimate enterprise, give ethnography its vitality, its reach, and its peculiar strength. Like jazz, ethnography has established deep intellectual roots, attracting scholars and practitioners from a variety of fields and a kaleidoscope of backgrounds. And like jazz, ethnography continues to defy strict or easy demarcation. Ethnographers might well echo Louis Armstrong's sentiments when he was asked to define jazz, and responded, "I know it when I hear it."

Ethnography has a "commonsense" and "commonplace" aspect to it which both simplifies and problematizes it (McDermott, 1977). The "common place" of ethnography can be illustrated by looking at how each of us behaves when we try to understand unusual or different behavior in context. A graduate student in psychology, for example, attending her first professional meeting, might feel strange as she goes from session to session hearing speaker after speaker present papers, only to have each paper formally criticized or even attacked at its conclusion by a colleague of the original speaker. Her unfamiliarity with this type of scholarly behavior forces the graduate student to attend to details, reflect on experiences, pick up patterns, and construct possible explanations. At first she hypothesizes an angry disagreement over research agendas and methods, then a kind of posturing and ritualizing. As the unfamiliar becomes more common she begins to see the meeting as the insiders see it—as time to exchange ideas, information, and work; an opportunity to sharpen and clarify perspectives; a networking occasion and a social gathering. Making sense out of an initially bewildering cultural or social form is the "common place" of ethnography.

Since we all do this all the time, isn't ethnography just as ordinary as mud? What makes an ethnographer different from, say, our graduate student? Answering these questions will help to clarify how the "common sense" and the "common place" of ethnography complicate as well as simplify. Recognizing that we have all had experiences similar to those of the graduate student is useful in that it helps to demystify ethnography, to bring it closer to us. But the experience described above no more makes the graduate student an ethnographer than the ability to whistle a little improvised tune while fishing, say, makes me a jazz musician.

What is missing in both instances is rigor and discipline. The ethnographer is immersed in a field of study in a self-conscious way. An educational ethnographer, for example, is assumed to be a scholar in the world of schools. The ethnographer is someone who is both aware of the current literature in the field and capable of interacting productively with the literature as well as with the field of study, the school settings themselves. Further, it is possible that the background and skill of the researcher make her or him something of an "educational connoisseur" (Eisner, 1977), a person of subtlety and grace in relation to looking into schools. In any case the educational ethnographer must apply knowledge, personal biography, experience, training, and talent to the complex process of inquiry, and therefore is assumed to possess precisely those qualities.

Furthermore, the ethnographic inquiry must be rigorous and disciplined. Information can be gathered using a variety of means, but the method of gathering information must be made explicit. Hervé Varenne (1986) makes this point succinctly when he argues that "rigor in ethnography consists in clarifying the position of the ethnographer" (p. 1). In other words, while our graduate student collects a lot of information, some of it haphazardly and some of it more deliberately, she does not, generally speaking, sort through the information systematically, nor does she explicitly account, to herself or anyone else, for how she gathered her information or how she warrants her conclusions, something required of the ethnographer. Hers is an informal affair freely mixing insight with prejudice, feeling with knowing. She is nowhere accountable to sort it out.

Michael Agar (1980) describes ethnographic rigor in terms of personal consciousness and makes the point somewhat more fully:

> The problem is not whether the ethnographer is biased; the problem is what kind of biases exist—how do they enter into ethnographic work and how can their operation be documented. By bringing as many of them to consciousness as possible, an ethnographer can try to deal with them as part of methodology and can acknowledge them when drawing conclusions during analysis. In this sense, ethnography truly is a personal discipline as well as a professional one. (pp. 41–42.)

As part of the personal discipline involved in preparing the portraits in this book, I constructed my autobiography, which helped me gain insights into my own biases. It is presented as Appendix A so that the reader can be acquainted with them as well.

Sarah Lawrence Lightfoot (1983) turns the problem of bias into a strength of ethnographic inquiry:

> It is not only that qualitative research uses "the person" as the research tool, the perceiver, the selector, the interpreter, and that one must always guard against the distortions of bias and prejudice; it is also that one's personal style, temperament, and modes of interaction are central ingredients of successful work. Phenomenologists often refer to the "inter-subjectivity" required in qualitative inquiry—the need to experience and reflect upon one's own feelings in order to successfully identify with another's perspective. Empathic regard, therefore, is key to good data collection. (p. 370)

The ethnographer, then, analyzes information formally, rigorously, and explicitly. An ethnographic account, the product of the fieldwork, must be more than recordings of observations and interviews, and it must be more than one's own feelings of what makes sense about something new or strange. The report must reflect an attempt on the part of the ethnographer to bring data under control, so to speak, to create a frame through which information can be understood. This is sometimes called inventing theory or discovering theory or grounding theory in reality (Glaser & Strauss, 1967). What it means simply is that a local or small theory is generated to account for as much of the observed activity or behavior as possible, rather than the more traditional approach of looking at reality in an attempt to confirm or deny a previously generated grand theory. Ethnographers contrast the "experimental hypothesis" generated prior to the concrete work of inquiry, with the "ethnographic hypothesis" that arises from the fieldwork itself and is generated during and after the process of inquiry (Overholt & Stallings, 1976).

The goal of ethnography is, therefore, not prediction but understanding. Ethnography is best at analytical description, or "better" description, and it is worst at prophecy. Reading a case study, like reading a novel, may offer the reader valuable insights about human beings, about pattern as well as about idiosyncracy and specificity, but what one learns is not necessarily generalizable. Richard Schweder (1988) argues that what makes some ethnographies outstanding is that, like poetry, the "texts bind us to a reality by presenting themselves as examples of the reality they describe" (p. 13). There can be insight and example without forecast. Like the linguist who can write a grammar from speaking with only one or two people but cannot predict how many—indeed, if anyone beyond that one or two—speak that language, the ethnographer can perceive patterns but cannot generalize from them. In this sense, conclusions are generalizable existentially, but not statistically. To the positivist this represents a serious flaw; to the ethnographer it affirms a particular world view.

The successful use of ethnography in educational research is difficult in part because schools, after all, are such familiar territory. The educational ethnographer must make a special effort to bracket the common sense, to suspend the known, to be open to surprise, to perceive the familiar in an unfamiliar way, to see the everyday with eyes wide open. Further, the educational ethnographer must be clear about position, history, and biography in relation to the study. In this way readers can make their own judgments about the validity and usefulness of the ethnographic account.

Given the dangers and the difficulties, there are a variety of reasons to pursue ethnographic inquiry in educational research. Schools and classrooms are complex settings, places where isolating particular variables or behaviors can be more mystifying than clarifying. As Eliot Eisner (1977) argues, "The range, richness, and complexity of educational phenomena occurring within classrooms are wider than can be measured. Some phenomena can only be rendered" (p. 5).

The school culture (Sarason, 1982) and ethos (Rutter et al., 1979), for example, are intricate, intertwined dimensions of school life that are all but impossible to pinpoint in a quantifiable way, and yet exert powerful influences in specific settings. Ethnographic research can be helpful in unearthing and making comprehensible these kinds of important dimensions. Ethnography can help us develop a common language in educational research, one that should be an aid in overcoming the pervasive problem described by Smith and Keith (1971):

> At this point in time, professional education, both as a science and as an art, remains so much a personal kind of experience that it is difficult to talk productively about it without having common concrete experience. The language is very inexplicit and carries so many multiple referents for each term that it is not until one is in the concrete situation that the intended meanings become clear. (p. 381)

"Making sense" of a social activity or cultural pattern is the standard by which ethnography is measured. This brings us to another level of understanding what it is we do when we "do ethnography." Culture has perhaps as many definitions as there are anthropologists, but most would endorse Clifford Geertz's (1973) definition as an embarkation point:

> Believing, with Max Weber, that man [sic] is an animal suspended in webs of significance he himself has spun, I take culture to be those webs, and the analysis of it to be therefore not an experimental science in search of law but an interpretive one in search of meaning. (p. 5)

Geertz amplifies the concept of thick description proposed by Gilbert Ryle, by discussing Ryle's account of "two boys rapidly contracting the eyelids of their right eyes." As the chronicle unfolds, it turns out that one of the boys is twitching, while the other boy is winking. Even though the mechanical movement is identical, and any purely technical descriptions of the physical gesture would be indistinguishable from each other, anyone watching the two could differentiate the winker from the twitcher. Anyone, that is, endowed with the same cultural antennae. When a third boy joins the drama, this time parodying the winker, or perhaps the twitcher, we see a complex chain of possibilities from mockery to intrigue to satire, and we begin to see the value of "thick descriptions" in a search for intention and significance.

Because people construct meaning in intricate and knotty ways, understanding meaning requires engagement with complexity. It involves observation of action and behavior, but it also includes observation of background and context. It involves noting conduct and production, but it also implies the discovery of significance. It is necessarily broad and interpretive. Seymour Sarason (1982) has this in mind when he discusses the impossibility, for example, of an outsider understanding what a first baseman does in a baseball game, by focusing exclusive attention on the first baseman. A more useful approach might be to study everyone else, the first baseman's actions having significance only in relation to the broader context.

Of course more is at stake in this discussion than winks, twitches, and baseball players. There is a distinct danger in social science inquiry of narrowing our gaze for the sake of utility, but in the process doing violence to our ability to understand. Take the example of an educational researcher who was studying negative teacher–student interaction and its impact on student achievement. In this study the researcher created an instrument, a checklist, to record negative teacher–student interactions. As it turned out, identical checks occurred in situations where a teacher reprimanded a student, abused a student verbally, and slammed a student against the wall, threatening to break his arm. The intensity and significance of these differences were washed out as "negative teacher–student interaction." People and their behaviors were aggregated in the interest of tidy answers, but the richness of reality, including feeling, intention, and significance, was entirely lost.

When the positivist paradigm, which rumbles more or less comfortably in the inanimate world of things and objects, is conveyed intact to the world of human beings, we create unbridgeable gaps and insurmountable problems. To talk of people is precisely to talk of subjects, and to talk of subjects is to talk of minds and intentions, emotions and values. Subjectivity is not a dirty word when subjects are the objects of study. And no matter how they are chopped, dissected, stripped, and sorted, people are always subjects and never things. Jean Paul Sartre (1966) argues that consciousness resists objectification, and that it is the essence of consciousness to be subject. When social scientists look about them and see only small and scripted lives, when they place themselves above or outside the contexts in which we all exist, or fail to extend their own undeniable (albeit difficult to prove) experience of free choice and imagination and subjectivity to others, they run the risk of denying their very reason for being: that is, clearer, deeper, and thicker understanding of people like themselves, of subjects.

## Autobiography

Autobiography is the recent invention of a specific cultural moment, the word developing in the late eighteenth century from the Greek words meaning "self-life-writing." "Autobiography" was subsequently used to describe an existing literature known variously as memoirs, confessions, recollections, and life histories. Autobiography has become the genre of choice not only of the famous and the powerful but of a wide range of "ordinary" people, and reading other people's stories has increasingly become a national pastime.

Peter Berger (1963) ties the interest in autobiography to the accelerating social, geographic, and political mobility characterizing society. It is this mobility, he claims, that leads people to autobiography as an explanation and justification of whom one has become. Autobiography in this view is a response to the flux, motion, chaos, and noise of the environment, something Berger calls a "global historical phenomenon" and "a real existential problem in the life of the individual" (p. 65). Autobiography is an attempt to ground oneself and explain oneself in the whirlwind.

Of course any attempt by people to verbalize their experience results in a kind of fiction. Any ordering, any metaphor, any choice of angle limits even as it illuminates. This is why every work requires a reader, a subject who completes the work through satisfaction and a sense of fulfilling the intentional circle (Mandel, 1980). The reader in a sense releases the truth of a work by choosing what piece to look at, what truth to seek. In other words, the reader chooses fiction knowing there will be truths of possibility, and chooses autobiography knowing there will be falsehoods in the explained life. The reader lets the work speak, and must be present to the work in order to co-create its truth or falsity.

Mandel further describes autobiography as a "passage to truth, because like all genuine experience, it rises from a ground of being that transcends one's memories, petty lies, grand deceptions, and even one's desire to be honest" (p. 64). He points out that while "the past may appear to rule the present," it is the opposite that is true: "All genuine power resides in the moment of creativity" (p. 64). "Ratification" of a past, then, is essentially the disclosure of the truth of the present. When I describe my childhood, for example, as happy and full, I am speaking as a son, but also as a father and a teacher today. An entirely different authentic voice might have stressed a fuller sense of alienation from my upbringing had I written an autobiographical narrative at 18. The point is that both accounts can be honest if the "illusion of the past [is] put forward in good faith" (p. 66).

Madeleine Grumet (1978) develops a method of teacher autobiography, for supervisory purposes, noting that "autobiography, like teaching, combines two perspectives, one that is a distanced view—rational, reflective, analytic, and one that is close to its subject matter—immediate, filled with energy and intention" (p. 212). For Grumet, autobiography establishes the legitimacy of the teachers' own questions, their "stories, reminiscences of grade school, travel, family relationships, tales of humiliation, triumph, confusion, revelation" (p. 209). Autobiography also establishes a public record, the possibility for dialogue:

> When the stories are very general and muted they bury their questions in clichés and happy endings, and the supervisor's response is to ask for more detail. When the stories are extremely detailed, they often exclude any reference to the writer's response to the events that are chronicled as well as the meanings that have been drawn from them, and then the supervisor's approach is to ask what these meanings might be. (p. 209)

Peter Abbs (1974) further articulates the value of autobiography in education. He denounces teacher training as methods courses preoccupied with facts and techniques, and advocates instead a deeper model of education that could somehow relate being and knowing, existence and education. For this, Abbs sees a central role for autobiography:

> How better to explore the infinite web of connections which draws self and world together in one evolving gestalt than through the act of autobiography in which the student will recreate his [sic] past and trace the growth of his experience through lived time and felt relationships? What better way to assert the nature of true knowledge than to set the student ploughing the field of his own experience? . . . May he not discover that "education" [is] that action of the inward spirit, by which . . . one discovers who one is? (p. 6)

For Abbs, looking backward, clarifying the unclear, discovering the unknown creates the conditions for imagining a future different from today. Asking, "Who am I? How did I get here?" opens the door for asking "Who will I be? How will I get there?"

Teachers have a special responsibility for self-awareness, for clarity and integrity, because teachers are in such a powerful position to witness, influence, and shepherd the choices of others. In dialogue with a student, a teacher can "underscore his subjectness—encourage him to stand personally related to what he says and does" (Noddings, 1984, p. 178), but only if the teacher is aware of her own subjectness, able to stand personally related herself.

Autobiography then is an act of self-penetration and self-understanding. We recognize the presentness of the autobiographer, the way in which memories and recollections must have meaning for now, and how that meaning can help shape intentionality and wide-awakeness for the future. And we see that autobiography can be particularly salient for teachers who exist not only in the matrix of self and world but also at the crossroads of so many other biographies.

## Portraiture

Sarah Lawrence Lightfoot (1983) compares her work in studying high schools to the work of a portrait artist:

Artists must not view the subject as object, but as a person of myriad dimensions. The artist's gaze is discerning as it searches for the essence, relentless as it tries to move past the surface images. But in finding the underside, in piercing the cover, in discovering the unseen, the artist offers a critical and generous perspective—one that is both tough and giving. (p. 6)

Lightfoot links her method to her own compelling experience of having her portrait sketched and painted, of seeing herself brought to life on canvas, of seeing an image that looked to her both strange and familiar, shocking and recognizable, off in detail but accurate in essence. From this personal, autobiographical experience Lightfoot draws for her own work the lesson that

portraits capture essence: the spirit, tempo and movement of the young girl; the history and family of the grown woman . . . portraits tell you about parts of yourself about which you are unaware, or to which you haven't attended . . . portraits reflect a compelling paradox, of a moment in time and of timelessness . . . portraits make the subjects feel "seen" in a way they have never felt seen before, fully attended to, wrapped up in an empathetic gaze. (p. 5)

Lightfoot calls her methodology "portraiture," a poetic title for "a form of inquiry that would embrace many of the descriptive, aesthetic, and experiential dimensions that I had known as the artist's subject; that would combine science and art; that would be concerned with composition and design as well as description; that would depict motion and stopped time, history and anticipated future" (p. 6). Her work is guided by the ethnographic assumption that to be comprehended, schools must be seen in their broadest social-historical contexts. Schools are assumed to be complex places, places reflecting the weight of history, culture, ethos, social context, and biography, as well as bureaucracy, political reality, and administrative contingency. To understand schools, then, they must be captured in action, in motion, and in the ever-changing framework of the construction of personal meaning by the participants themselves. To study a piece of the school experience, to isolate a variable, to narrow one's gaze—these are precisely the things that kill so much of meaning and render a study less than useful.

Portraiture can become an act of telling and listening to each other's stories, an exercise in understanding our own social history. The telling of life stories gives us clues to the present as well as hints of the future. It provides the possibility of becoming more conscious, more intentional. Portraiture is, perhaps, particularly important in discussing something as complex, holistic, and immediate as teaching, something for which we lack an adequate, embracing language and so are confronted with the choice to "reduce the experience to the fractions of its wholeness or . . . talk about what it is like" (Denton, 1974, p. 107).

In a sense, the portraits in this book are informed by the feminist movement, in part because of the ways these six women have grown and changed in the modern context, and in part because the women's movement has raised the practice of telling one's own story and rendering a view of lived life to an art form. Consciousness-raising groups, the spontaneous and major organizational configuration of the women's movement, have evolved a unique epistemology, one based on personal accounts. The experienced, the felt, the lived are the sources of knowledge, the base upon which analysis, theory, and action are built. In this work as well, perspectives of these teachers were both subject and source. This is not a tactic, but essential to the study. Like Lightfoot's (1983) "empathetic regard," a sense of compassion and involvement is necessary in order to apprehend how people feel and face their teaching lives.

The autobiographical narratives are, of course, more than descriptions of facts and events. They are interpretations, chronicles of meaning, reconstructions of experiences in light of the present. They seek essential truths in lived lives. The narratives, at their best, reveal patterns and lead to generalizations, but they do not result in abstractions, which rely on "fractionalizing and subsumption" (Denton, 1974, p. 112). The auto-biographical narratives reach toward unity, coherence, and meaning for a subject in a moment. They are not assumed to be the last word, as Denton (1974) points out, "not because the number of variables is too great, the time too short, or the instruments inadequate, but because mystery can never be fully disclosed" (p. 113).

# ☆ 2 ☆

# ANNA
# The Other Mother

Anna Tiant has been an early childhood teacher for seventeen years, the last seven in infant and toddler care. She is married and has a seven-year-old daughter. Anna lives within a block of her mother, her grand-mother, and several aunts, uncles, and cousins.

When we think about day care, we often think about social welfare agencies and poor families. This is because the roots of day care stretch back through the settlement house movement in the early part of this century to the work of Maria Montessori on behalf of Italy's poor. The popularity of day care has been checkered, rising as a result of the action of women in the work force during World Wars I and II and again in modern times, falling with the rise of forces opposed to women working outside the home. Today, popular attitudes about day care are decidedly mixed: It is both desired and demanded, sought after and attacked. But one idea has shifted markedly: As the need for day care grows, there are fewer and fewer people who perceive day care as the unfortunate lot of the poor.

Affordable, convenient, high-quality child care is increasingly seen as something that should be the right of every child and the choice of every family. There is growing evidence of the long-term benefits to individual children as well as to society of quality early childhood programs. This, combined with the enormous demand for child care, is fueling dramatic changes, including the explosive growth in day-care programs for infants and toddlers. Infant care is the fastest growing component of the dramatically expanding world of child care.

Anna sits on the floor of the toddler room peek-a-boo-ing with Eliot, who is hiding under the ramp that leads to the low loft. His flexible 15-month-old body folds and fits neatly into this space. Eliot periodically pokes his head out, eyes riveted to Anna and face flushed with excited anticipation. "Boo!" Anna punctuates Eliot's peek with perfect harmony and Eliot explodes in squeals of delight. Eliot's joy and hilarity are contagious and Anna laughs too. Eliot pulls back into his hiding place, waits a moment and then bursts out once more. "Boo!" He squeals again and pulls back. This is such a clever game, making everything disappear and then suddenly appear again, to hold on to the image of the disappeared in his head and then to bring it back in reality. Such power! On and on they play, over a dozen peeks and boos. Eliot looks as if he could go on forever, but hard reality imposes in the form of a bumped head. His face opens in shock and then dissolves into tears and sobbing. Anna scoops him up and he molds to her, burying his face in her neck. "Okay," she says soothingly as she supports him and pats his back, swaying slightly. "Okay, Eliot. You bumped your head. Ouch! Okay." She coos and soothes, and in minutes Eliot is calmed and toddling off toward the water table, where Asha's splashing has caught his eye and interest.

"My job is to be a mother substitute," Anna says later. "I'm a teacher, yes. But a teacher of toddlers and babies is mostly a mother substitute. By that I mean that what's important to very young kids is to be loved, to be safe, to be cared for and that's what I do. The toddler curriculum is a curriculum of love and play. The first months of being away from your parents can be terribly difficult, and we try to tune in to each individual child, to learn from them, to understand them so that we can help them discover that they are safe and known and cared for here. Then they can go about being with other kids, finding their friends as well as the materials that will interest and encourage them because they are confident that this is their private space to be in, and that the adults here are their trusted friends."

Anna can remember and relive being a baby and a child—moods and feelings more than events or details. When she holds a child, she remembers that sense of safety that comes with being in the strong arms of a friendly giant. When she comforts a crying child, she remembers the wonderful sense of relief and well-being that can follow sadness, sorrow, falling apart. She remembers feeling her mother's presence when she opened her lunch at school and saw the way the sandwich was cut. She knows how it feels to lie on a fluffy rug and kick your feet, to be caressed by the ribbon on the edge of a soft blanket, to sleep on the rear window deck of a car returning home through the night.

Successful teachers remember; they are in touch with their childlikeness, which is also their basic humanity. They accept their own fear of separateness, understand their own struggle for independence, embrace their own ignorance and desire for competence. They have the capacity to look at things as a child sees them.

"Separation is a serious issue for me," says Anna. "As a very young child my parents separated and I was sent to Cuba to live with my grandmother. I'm very aware of the head and body symptoms of hard separation. As kids go through it, I go through it with them. I understand and feel it and try to bring them through it. I hold and reassure and comfort. Today, I wouldn't think of spending a weekend away from my daughter even though it's not overwhelming to her. I'd be completely reliving my own difficulties as a child. I'd be suffering the whole weekend."

"When I'm holding a child who's miserable at separating," says Sally, one of Anna's co-workers, "my heart is breaking and I can't stand it. It's so sad and I'm so unhappy. But when a parent is having a hard time separating, I can only sort of understand it. I don't understand their feeling guilty, I guess because it's me they're leaving the child with."

"Well, before I had my own child, I sometimes felt that parents were stupid and messed up," Anna says. "There was one woman who used to peek in the window every few minutes until, inevitably, her kid saw her and went berserk. I used to think she was a fool. I understand her pain better now.

"My grandmother in Cuba was very open and very loving," says Anna. "But of course I missed my mom. In school my brother and I were looked down on because we were black. And also, I'm left-handed and I had a sock tied to my hand in school. I was confused and pained. I remember wondering what was wrong with me that I was left-handed and black," she says, looking at her hand.

"Finally I told my grandmother and it turned out that she was left-handed too, and had had similar problems. She marched over to school and raised hell. I was treated much better after that. I don't know what she did, but it made me feel that she was strong and good and would take care of me. And also it made me know that I wasn't wrong or bad."

Anna was in Cuba when the revolution triumphed. She remembers being in the backyard one day and seeing people running, and her grandmother yelling to come in, and hearing rifle cracks and seeing a man fall in a pool of blood. This memory is a blur of violence and peril.

When she came back to the United States in 1962, she didn't know any English. She stayed close to her mother and brother, and they remain close to this day. "I learned English and I succeeded in school. But I remember seeing a nun put gum into a kid's hair as a punishment for chewing it in class, and I saw a Jesuit brother bang a boy's head repeatedly on a desk. I wondered why they were teachers since they hated us. And I remember realizing that really they didn't know what they were doing. They were completely insecure, emotionally arrested.

"Later I helped a friend take care of kids in her apartment. I wanted to be a teacher because I liked being with kids and I felt so many people didn't like them and it wasn't fair.

"Then in college I was assigned as a student teacher at a wonderful preschool. I stayed 10 years, until I had my daughter. I thought I wouldn't go back, but, you know, I'm a nurturing person. I need to teach to have purpose and meaning in my life."

Anna was born into a Roman Catholic culture but was also raised with an "island religion" called *Lucuimis*, which originated in the Yoruba tribe in Africa and was passed down through generations, slavery, and migrations. It is a spiritualism that is never taught but simply observed and practiced.

"Now everyone lives within a block of my house," Anna says. "I can see my mother's window from my apartment. My aunt is in the building; my cousins are a block away. I don't move without seeing someone in my family. A lot of people would go crazy, but for me it's wonderful."

Anna's room is arranged for toddlers—it invites exploration and inter-action at about two feet off the ground. In one corner is a low fenced-in loft accessible up a narrow ramp with a thick banister for pulling oneself along. The ramp itself seems to be the main attraction for many as they busily go up and down, passing one another with that penguin waddle familiar to toddlers, jockeying into position, creating and correcting little traffic jams at either end. They are practicing this exciting and important skill of walking. Others busy themselves in the loft itself, pulling dress-ups from cubbies, draping heads and shoulders with bits of material, pouring imaginary tea or juice, setting and clearing the tiny table. One child, 22 months old, is dialing the telephone with great interest and attention. He pauses, then speaks into the receiver, "Mommy?" Another pause. "Okay." Then again, "Mommy?" Pause. "Okay." He is thinking about separation and finding a way to cope with it through his play.

Near the loft is a blue, peak-roofed house cut from an extra-strong cardboard packing box. It has a door, three windows, and shutters, which provide a wonderful space for hiding and playing peek-a-boo.

Zach is watching the goldfish flit about in their aquarium. He touches the glass thoughtfully, then moves around to the other side and touches the glass again. Where are they? How do they get in and out? Zach watches for several minutes, circling the fish; finally he loses interest and walks off to join two kids stacking large, cardboard building blocks into towers, which inevitably crash to the ground as the seventh or eighth block is piled on. Alessia takes a block and pulls it over to the fish, where she sits on it like a chair and watches the fish intently as if they were a TV show.

Riding toys, a small slide, and a boat-rocker big enough for four chil-dren are parked at one end of a large open space. There are tables and chairs, easels and paint, and a transparent tub on short legs and full of brightly colored plastic cups in sudsy warm water. Max is at the water table, splashing, picking up a red cup and pouring the water over his fat little hand. Then he picks up a yellow one, pours out the water, and, as he does with most things, tries to pop it into his mouth. The cup is much too large so Max explores its edges, sucking and chewing.

The book corner is a large area defined by low cubbies, a book rack, a very long couch, and a thick piece of blue and white carpet that feels a bit like clouds and sky. As King Sunni Adé blows sweet musical sounds from the record player, Sally, Anna's co-worker, reads to four children who are piled upon and around her. Like piglets or puppies trying to find a comfortable place to nurse, these four clamor and crawl, squirm and squeal, adjust and readjust in a continuing chain reaction until interest in the business at hand, in this case listening to and looking at a book, arrests them and holds them momentarily suspended in the most unlikely poses, legs spread, arms akimbo or wrapped awkwardly around a neighboring limb, heads tilted, twisted, or bent. And then one seeks a better view, a less contorted position, and the whole organism moves and shakes and ripples again toward another momentary pause.

Sally is impervious, calm and relaxed, snuggling each one and reading along, delighting them with her voice and the sounds of the words. "One berry/Two berry/Pick me a blueberry." A barefoot child in overalls and straw hat cavorts through fields and waterfalls and piles of colorful berries with a large cuddly bear. "Hatberry/Shoeberry/In my canoeberry." Bessie points at the bear and says, "Berry!" "Raspberry/Jazzberry/Razzamatazzberry/Berryland/Merryland/Jamming in Berryland." All four children are laughing and touching the pictures. "Mountains and fountains/Rain down on me/Buried in berries/What a jam jamboree." Everyone slides off Sally's lap into a heap on the rug, laughing and shrieking in what looks like a ritualistic ending to this book. Three clamber back to her lap for another story while Asha toddles off toward the loft. Zach is sitting off by himself. His book is *You Go Away*, a picture book about separation and reunion.

"We don't read to kids out of any sense of pushing them to be precocious," Sally says. "We read to them because we value books and we see that they love to read. Partly they love to snuggle and to be held on a lap. Partly they love the pictures. And partly they love the language, they love to hear it, to play with it, to practice it. Getting familiar with a book at this age, being able to anticipate what's coming, is terrifically satisfying. Even these very young kids will fill in the last words in a sentence in a very familiar book. It's a game that delights them."

There are nine children in the group with Anna, Sally, and Lorraine, the third co-worker. A couple of the children are almost two and a couple are closer to one, but most are hovering around eighteen months old. They are busy, attentive, and active. Attempting to document the movements of two of them on a floor plan became scribble-scrabble inside of three minutes. They moved with speed and purpose. "Alessia walking around the room is not necessarily aimless," says Anna. "A large part of her work these days is the work of practicing walking. She's getting to know herself and the space around her. So she walks."

Anna, Sally, and Lorraine are in almost constant motion, often doing two or three things at once, twirling, spinning, dancing. An Ode to Toddlers: bending to tie a shoe, scooping someone up to change a diaper, soothing the hurt, holding a hand, cleaning up the snack, picking up a discarded book, putting out the cots, bending, stretching, moving. *Port de Bras. Plié. Battement Tendu.*

"It's exhausting work," admits Anna. "But it's much more emotionally draining than physically exhausting, because you have to be tuned in to some very important and basic human needs all the time. I try to keep things in perspective, to remind myself to focus on the kids themselves. 'Okay,' I say, 'the water table gets dumped, we'll have to clean it up. I'll get the mop.' I get my own anxiety out of the way, because nothing is worth the agitation and hysteria."

Or perhaps these teachers are like the cartoon characters stretching to put every finger and toe in the dike as hole after hole appears. But no, because the rhythm of the group is such that the dike never really breaks. The energy changes. Refocuses. They sit and sing. Or bring out paint or clay or food. They move ahead.

"It also helps that we have a team of teachers," says Anna. "We need each other. We can step back from something that's difficult to deal with and help each other out. You need to have a supportive, communicating staff. It's a bit like a good marriage, having someone to share the joy and also the problems, someone to bounce the emotions off of."

In a group of nine toddlers no teacher can love or even know each one well, even though each has a right to be loved and understood. Nor will every child respond positively to a single teacher. The chance of this important toddler-caregiver relationship being productive and successful increases dramatically when there is a team of like-minded teachers who see the importance of each individual child. The implications of this extend to three- or six- or twelve-year-old children in our schools, who are too often in groups of ten or twenty or forty with a single teacher.

The notion that babies and young children are passive blobs of inactivity has been demolished in recent years by the findings of Mahler, Piaget, Erikson, Bruner, and others. We know that children work hard to find meaning in their experiences and that they are constantly creating and recreating cognitive and psychological models in which to fit their discoveries. What to an uninformed observer may look like a world of chaos and mindlessness is to the child the serious work of creating a personal existence. Recent studies indicate that babies learn a good deal *in utero,* and pregnant women have told us that their unborn babies respond to certain foods, to rock music, to a bumpy ride, to mother's moods. Babies are born curious and are driven by a deep internal desire to know and to become competent. The active baby, sucking, staring, tensing, stiffening, is soon sitting, creeping away, pulling, crawling, and then walking, talking, exploring, practicing, toddling. From the day of birth the baby sets out to conquer the world.

"Do you want some Play-Doh, Alessia?" Anna is sitting at a table on a toddler-sized chair with a blob of blue in front of her. Alessia shrieks and runs to the table laughing. She sits down, and Anna breaks off a little piece for each one of them. "Here's a piece for you and one for me. What are you going to do with that little piece?"

Alessia pounds the Play-Doh hard, watching it flatten out under her blows. She is smiling, her tongue sticking slightly out of the corner of her mouth. Her face is relaxed and her eyes sparkle. Finally the flattened Play-Doh comes apart into two pieces. Alessia frowns and says, "Uh oh!"

"Uh oh," repeats Anna. "What happened?"

"Uh oh," says Alessia again, her eyes moving sadly from the dough to Anna and back to the squished dough.

"Well, Alessia, it broke," says Anna. "Now you have two pieces."

Parents know that the line between communicating and talking is a fine one. Babies and toddlers communicate with their bodies, their hands, their faces, their cries, their eyes. Parents respond by holding, changing, rocking, walking, patting—by letting the baby know that they understand. In this way babies and parents create and recreate and carry on a dialogue. Confidence in that early communication leads to confidence in subsequent communications and has tremendous implications for all areas of growth and development.

Early communication is also supplemented with words and with a tone of voice that says, "I understand." Mothers coo and babble, imitate and model, and play the games that every generation of babies invents anew: "Peek-a-boo," "Where's mommy?" "Surprise," "Chase." Anna responds to Alessia's babbles and grunts and groans, sometimes guessing, often knowing, what she means. Anna's response encourages Alessia to keep on and feeds her desire toward ever more effective communication.

As Alessia scrapes her dough back into a ball, three more children arrive at the table and Anna quickly seats each one in front of a blob of blue Play-Doh. Alessia stamps her feet and shrieks, scowling at Asha nearest her, her face stuck out in challenge. Anna touches Alessia lightly on the arm and says, "It's okay. We have enough Play-Doh for everyone." Alessia pulls her head back in, smiles tentatively, and pounds her Play-Doh once very hard with her fist. Bang! Asha laughs and imitates, pounding her own piece. Bang! Now Alessia is glad for the company and pounds her dough even harder to general approval. Bang! Bang! She smiles all around the table, then closes her eyes, takes a deep breath, and issues forth a high-pitched piercing scream. Asha, Eliot, and Max roar with laughter and bob up and down in their chairs. Alessia howls, delighted with herself. When the general hilarity dies down slightly, Eliot closes his eyes and shrieks. *Eeeee!* The rest squeal with delight, bobbing up and down again. Each in turn repeats this neat trick several times. *Eeeee! Eeeee!* Interest slowly returns to the Play-Doh. Several more children arrive and join in the work; others move on to different things.

Zach bounds over to the table, and Alessia unexpectedly tears off a blue piece and hands it to him, smiling. Zach takes the piece, not acknowledging the person connected to the offering hand, and begins pushing and pulling. Anna says, "Thank you for sharing with Zach, Alessia."

Zach pushes his finger into and through the dough, making a hole. He holds up his piece and looks directly at Anna and says, "Ha!" Anna smiles and says, "Good, Zach. You put your finger right through it." Bessie pushes her finger through her blob of dough, holds it up, and says, "Ha!"

"Oh, you did it too," says Anna. "Look, Bessie put her finger through too." Bessie extends her arm, turning her hand for all to see, and beams at the misshapen blue blob with her index finger poking through.

Anna gets some flour from a large canister. "The Play-Doh's a little wet," she explains. "We'd better add some more flour." She puts a handful of flour in front of each child. "Flour!" exclaims Bessie. "Flour, flour!" says Asha. Clouds of flour and happy shrieks fill the air as satisfied little fists pound the dough. Anna says, "Don't eat it, Bluejay. If you're hungry I'll get you a cracker." Bluejay's face is powdered white from forehead to chin. He blinks twice and says seriously, "Play-Doh." He looks up at Anna with a wide wet smile, saliva drooling in two separate streams from his mouth. "Play-Doh." He looks absolutely comical, and Anna laughs and says, "You've got Play-Doh, Bluejay. Right, it's Play-Doh." She turns to Sally and says excitedly, "Another first, Sally. Bluejay said 'Play-Doh.'" Sally comes over and sits at the table. "Did you say 'Play-Doh,' Bluejay?" She pokes him gently with her finger. "Play-Doh," he says and everyone laughs. He's on a roll. "Play-Doh! Play-Doh!"

Bessie reaches to take some small pieces of dough from in front of Alessia. Alessia shrieks in protest, bares her teeth in a threatening gesture, and leans toward Bessie's arm. Anna moves quickly and effortlessly between Alessia and Bessie, reaches out again, and touches Alessia gently on the shoulder. "Here's some for you," she says to Bessie, gathering up a blob of dough. "And here's yours, Alessia. Don't bite; it hurts." Both children return to punching and pulling the dough.

Biting is one form of aggression that sets off intense, almost uncontrollable reactions in many adults, as memories and fantasies reverberate inside. Children at this age bite for a variety of reasons: They're teething and need to bite, they're still putting everything in their mouths, they're frustrated at being on the verge of talking yet still unable to use the strong, powerful words they need to describe their powerful feelings. It's important to provide a safe place for all children, important too to understand and acknowledge the needs of the biting child as well as of the victim. This is not easy, but it is an issue for all programs with very young children.

"In some ways I guess this is a hard age to be in a group," Anna says later. "They're all so self-centered. But in other ways this is a good time to learn about others in relation to yourself. Alessia may bite or hit or push. We say, 'No, you can't do that. It hurts!' We comfort the victim and may involve Alessia in comforting too. But then when she's hit or pushed, we say and do the same things. We show each kid respect and even-handedness. Over time they see that we insist on a safe, happy environment for everyone and that we demand respect and fairness for each one."

Conflict and anger are a natural and expected part of a preschool classroom. Children at this age will often fight against any real or imagined encroachment on their autonomy or their possessions. They are discovering their own borders and they may often feel compelled to defend their budding, separate selves. Frustration, defiance, aggression, rage, and regression are all part of the natural growth and behavior of toddlers.

"I avoid the question of who's right and who's wrong in a conflict," says Anna. "I don't want winners and losers. Problems arise between two kids because they're both absolutely right. Eliot was sitting on the red chair 15 minutes ago, but he got up to read with Sally. Now Asha's sitting on it. To Asha, it's her chair and Eliot ran over and pushed her off for no reason. What should a teacher do? To me, both have an absolute claim, both are absolutely right. So we need to anticipate conflict and to avoid it where possible—get enough chairs or Play-Doh or rice cakes or whatever—and we need to affirm and support each child's needs even as we help direct their energy into acceptable channels. We model sharing for them. We're a group. We share everything: food, possessions, space, love, attention, everything. And this we show them over time."

Lorraine is standing next to Bluejay while he paints at the easel. Big brush strokes of blue and yellow and red and then into his mouth: "Don't eat the paint, Bluejay," says Lorraine, gently mopping his face with a paper towel. "If you're hungry I'll get you a rice cake." Bluejay smiles a red-toothed smile at her and goes back to painting on paper. He pulls the painting from the easel, and Lorraine takes it and clips on a clean piece of paper. Bluejay paints again, watching with interest as thick gobs of color appear, brush across the paper, taper down, or drip and run. A few strokes and he pulls this painting off too, and Lorraine quickly but easily takes it with one hand and snaps on a clean piece with the other.

Alessia pushes a doll in a tiny stroller nearby. She stops suddenly and bends at the middle slightly. The color in her face deepens, her eyes tear up, and she looks off distantly. She stands frozen for several seconds, then relaxes and calls to Anna, "Diaper."

"Okay, Alessia," Anna comes over and picks her up. "Let's change that diaper." Anna picks up the doll and hands it to Alessia, then carries them both to the changing table.

The changing table is built into the wall next to the sink. It's two feet wide and waist high. Above it is a rack with neatly stacked diapers, paper towels, powder, cream, and oil. Anna lies Alessia on her back on the mat and unbuckles her overalls and begins to change her. "Is that your baby?" she asks. "Babe, babe," says Alessia smiling. "That's a nice baby," says Anna. "Does she drink a bottle?" "Baba." "When she's grumpy, you give her something to eat. And sometimes she takes a nap, and you sing to her." Anna sings a couple of lines. "Hush little baby, don't say a word, mama's gonna buy you a mocking bird. . . ." Alessia is holding the doll away from her, examining her and poking at her face with one finger. "And sometimes I'll bet you change her diaper," Anna says as she buckles up Alessia's overalls and lifts her down to the floor. Alessia runs off to the little stroller.

While loving children is an essential qualification for preschool teachers, it's inadequate as the single and defining qualification. Loving children in general is no help when dealing with nine or nineteen or twenty-nine flesh-and-blood children. What happens when someone is changing her fortieth diaper of the day? Or when a teacher meets a child she doesn't love? Or when she is in an unlovely situation where the children are treating neither her nor one another well? What good does abstractly loving idealized children do her then?

"Teachers need to know how to deal with people," Anna says. "They need to be psychologists and counselors and social workers. They need to love kids, and that means knowing how to meet their needs. It could be kissing or holding, or just smiling across the room, or it could be getting out the paint or changing wet clothes. You actively seek their cues and respond to the real people they are. When you love kids you are giving to them in specific ways, and you don't demand things back. You don't say, 'I'll give you this, if you'll do that.' Rather, you communicate that they are loved and lovable as they are, and you allow them to grow into trusting their own feelings." Anna laughs and adds, "And incidentally you do get a lot of love and affection back."

Anna feeds and changes and nurtures when that is what she feels is needed, but she also admires and respects the child's development toward self-reliance. She loves the child enough to hold it close, but also enough to let go when the child is ready to fly free. She meets the infant's needs, but she does not infantilize the toddler; she is mature enough to remember deep within the desire to be held but also the desire to run off. She supports the vulnerable child but that does not blind her to the durable and resilient child. She kisses and caresses, but she is also electrified by a child's development; as the child grows, finishing a project or reading a book can be a clearer expression of love than holding or kissing. It's a matter of sensitivity to the rhythm of love as a longing for liberty as well as connection.

"Loving kids means I want to physically take care of them, make them safe and comfortable," Sally says. "And also, I enjoy being with them. I enjoy their personalities. I like this age especially because I love watching them learn to walk and talk. It's so formidable, so awesome, that it keeps me going through some of the rougher times. They take off so fast, and then they're gone. It's mind-boggling, and it gives me a lot of hope."

Alessia and Max are bringing sponges to clean up the spilled juice at the table. Their bodies lean forward, heads out, feet just barely catching up, as they waddle onward. They look like chickens, Alessia bow-legged, swinging one leg in a great semi-circle and then planting her foot in an exaggerated pigeon-toed direction, picking up the other leg and swinging it in a long arc as well, and so on; Max taking short, rapid jab steps, his feet like wings pointing outward. Both move quickly across the floor, and what they lack in efficiency and grace they more than make up in glee. Cluck, cluck!

Eliot runs by on a mission to the book corner. His run is like a giraffe's, each separate part spinning and wheeling in the most unlikely relationship to any other part. It looks doubtful that Eliot will arrive without a thunderous fall into a confused heap of arms and legs. His face aims pointedly, determinedly at his destination. His neck is stretched forward, his feet are flying. He is moving fast. Meanwhile Bessie is running diagonally across the room in the other direction with her tiny quick steps, holding a doll in her hands, arms extended. She is looking into the doll's face saying, "Hi, hi! Hi!" Bessie and Eliot pass within inches of one another, miraculously missing a tremendous crash, and each moves on seemingly unaware of the narrowly averted disaster. "Hi! Hi!"

"When I watch them take their first steps," says Sally, "and then spend so much time and effort practicing this new and wonderful skill, I think that never again in life will they work so hard on something and at the same time get such pleasure from it."

The excitement of the new walker is palpable and it's so clearly an inner thing. There's nothing that a parent or teacher could offer that's more powerful than this drive to learn and master. When you watch a child fall again and again, bang her head and cut her chin, spin and lose control and come crashing down hard and then get up a hundred, two hundred, three hundred times, keep going until it is accomplished, and then spend hours and hours practicing, walking, running, climbing, it becomes apparent that the wellspring of learning and growth is within.

Babies learn to creep and crawl and walk. Parents marvel, laugh, encourage, comfort, and watch. On the success of these early experiences children build their bodies and their minds and their emotions. The current popularity of walkers, little seats and harnesses on wheels that allow baby to sit upright and wheel around the room, is misguided and potentially destructive to children. Whatever convenience walkers offer, they also short-circuit the crucial crawling stage, with negative implications for discovering body borders, eye-hand coordination, upper-body development, and successful exploration of the environment. They interfere with that peculiarly human evolutionary step of getting up off all fours onto our hind legs. Children of walkers can often be spotted at age three or four or five because their shoulders and chests are less developed, and they balance awkwardly on the balls of their feet instead of on the whole foot, firmly planted.

"I don't even like strollers," says Anna as she lifts Bessie into the oversized wagon they use for outings. "I know that they're convenient and necessary sometimes, but I think they're overused. Kids need to practice walking. They need the freedom to know their body's capabilities and limitations. We all need the exercise. If you use a stroller to get your kid to day care, so you can get to work on time, okay. But then maybe on the way home take a slow walk."

The group is going to the park. Six children are sitting in the wagon facing each other on high benches, strapped in with seat belts; three children are holding hands, walking. "I like them to make a choice between walking and the wagon. I think making these kinds of decisions helps them learn to make other decisions later on. These kids are mostly new walkers and they get tired. We need the wagon so an outing doesn't become a forced march. On the other hand we want to allow them to practice because walking is fun for them. The wagon's nice because they can see everything, they don't have to be down at the curbside with all the exhaust, and also they can talk or babble to each other. They can interact."

As they are ready to go, Zach reaches over and unzips Bluejay's jacket and they both laugh. Jamilya and Alessia are leaning forward, holding hands.

Nine children are sitting at the table having a snack: apple juice and apple slices, crackers and cream cheese. Asha takes a bite of apple, chews, drooling and smiling and watching the others. Slowly the apple peel, stripped of meat, is expelled in a long, neat roll. She's like a juicing machine, the juice and pulp go one way, the peel another.

Some kids are drinking from cups with tops and little drinking lips, halfway between a bottle and a cup, but not Bluejay. He's drinking from a cup in the most interesting way. He holds it up at eye level and tips it slowly until a small stream of juice starts running onto the table. He watches intently, then moves his mouth into the stream as one would with a drinking fountain. Lucian pours his juice carefully onto his cracker on the table, his head bent toward the action. He makes a damp cracker and a neat little puddle. He stirs the puddle thoughtfully with his forefinger, smiles, and runs to the sink for a sponge. He hurries back and mops up the mess, sits down and repeats the whole process.

Sally, sitting with them, asks, "Do you want more juice in your cup?" The word "cup" starts a chain reaction. Eliot says: "gup, gup, gup, gup." He shrieks the word in a rapid-fire manner, popping the "p" sound with relish. At the same time, Alessia raises her eyebrows and turns her head back and forth, rhythmically asking, "Cup? Cup? Cup?"

Anna says to Jamilya, "Drink your apple juice." And again there is a chorus: ajewss, ajewss, ajewss—goosh, goosh, goosh.

These children love to hear their own voices. They are playing with sounds and words all the time, and it gives them obvious pleasure. Without being taught words, and without ever being corrected, they are working away at language, correcting themselves, growing, accomplishing. The teachers don't talk baby talk, nor is their tone condescending. "We talk all the time," Anna says, "because they need language stimulation to develop what's there. But we don't talk down to them. I remember people talking down to me, and I didn't like it. Part of me is still a kid, and I find it painful to have people treat kids that way. I don't even talk to my dog the way I hear people talk to kids."

Sitting at the snack table one hears babbling children, with an occasional understandable word, and adults responding as if in a normal dialogue: "Yes, you can have one." "Okay, here's another cup." "We'll do it later, Alessia." "Zach, your cracker is over there." And again a chorus: cracker, cracker, cracker—cack, cack, cack.

"Of course you have to be with a young kid a lot to know what her body movements mean, what her facial expressions mean," Anna says. "But eventually you learn."

The snack table is calm and focused, but calm with toddlers is momentary and passing, and it will soon be split and broken by the real needs of young children. Still, for the moment, Anna and Sally look completely relaxed. Zach begins shaking his head wildly back and forth, laughing, enjoying the feel of his hair swinging. He stops, and four other children laugh with him. Jamilya and Bessie shake wildly and laugh. Alessia delights in the feeling of her hair whipping her neck and cheeks. She keeps on after the others have finished, now laughing quietly to herself at each pause in the action.

Lucian says to Sally, "I'm done." "Okay, put your cup in the garbage." "I'm not done." "Okay." "I'm done. I'm not going to eat it." "Okay, Lucian, whatever." "Yes, I'm going to eat it." Sally laughs.

Young children are often negative. They fight, have tantrums, refuse to eat or go to the toilet. "No!" "I do it myself." Sometimes their negativism seems to defeat their own purposes. But from the child's point of view, negativism is not all negative. Saying "no" to the world is also a way of saying "yes" to oneself. It is a way of affirming one's own autonomy, control, purpose. It is a way of clarifying and understanding one's own feelings.

Anna says, "Okay, Jamilya, Sally's getting you another cracker. She's getting more, Bessie." And again, the toddler chorus: More! More! More!

"This is a child-centered room," says Anna. "It's geared to their needs and desires. It's a room that supports them and responds to them, that stimulates them without overstimulating them. It's a place where kids can be together and it's just their size. There are all kinds of stacking and sorting toys for them to master. There are materials for big-muscle activities. And there's lots of time and space and materials that suggest fantasy play. There's a dress-up area, blocks, paint, and water. The curriculum is them. My job is to be motherly. I try to provide a continuity of affection and responsiveness."

Sally tapes big sheets of heavy brown paper to the table, while Anna takes off every child's outer clothing. "We're going to make hand prints," Sally says as the kids scramble into chairs around the table. Each child gets a paper plate with a shallow pool of red or blue or yellow paint in it.

Just as they are about to begin, Asha arrives with her mother and squeals a joyful greeting. Her tiny face is beaming from under layers of coat and hat and hood and scarf. "Hi! Hi!" she shouts and a chorus of Hi! Hi! Hi! erupts from the table. It's the one word they all pronounce exactly the same. As her mother unbundles her, Zach and Bessie run to her, smiling. Hi! Hi! Zach touches her arm and Bessie hugs her mother's legs.

Unbundled, Asha runs to the table shouting, "Me! Me!" Just as she arrives Alessia sticks her hand out hard, and Asha, like a halfback straight-armed, falls over. She springs up undaunted and goes wide around Alessia to Sally, shouting, "Me! Me!" "Here's a chair for you, Asha. And here's some paint. We're making hand prints." Asha sticks both hands into the paint. Her mother comes over and says good-bye to Asha, who glances up and then dives into her work.

Lucian is printing carefully in red, one hand pressed down, then the other. Bluejay is going rapidly from plate to paper using blue, of course, and then into his mouth. "Don't eat it, Bluejay," says Anna. "This is only for painting. If you're hungry I'll get you an apple." Jamilya is pounding with both hands in yellow and then smearing it back and forth. She shrieks with joy. Lucian says, "Look! Look!" He has made two perfect hand prints. Anna says, "Beautiful, Lucian. Those are very red hands."

Alessia sits straight and watches the others with a look of sour disapproval. Her head moves slowly from one to another, her frown deepening with each messy display of spontaneity. At last her eyes turn to the plate of blue in front of her. Still frowning she puts her right index finger tentatively into the paint. She spreads it slowly on the paper. Having thus begun, she smiles slightly and puts her whole hand in. She presses it on the paper, looks at it with interest, then looks at her blue-colored hand. She looks carefully around the table, more neutral this time, gets up, and goes to the sink to wash up.

Not every arrival and separation is as smooth as this one of Asha's. Jarel often cries and screams when his mother leaves, reaches out after her, and then sits passively near the door for a long time, glancing at it occasionally. A caregiver holds him and soothes him, assures him that she will take care of him, that his mother's working, and that she'll return after his nap. Even after Jarel is engaged in play and activity, if he is frustrated or angry, he goes to his cubby and watches the door. When his mother returns Jarel rarely embraces her. Rather, he stares angrily at her, or he hits and kicks her. Sometimes he turns to the unfortunate child nearest him and scratches or bites.

Each day around 10 AM the whole toddler group gathers on the floor in the book corner for Circle. There is a shifting pile on laps and rug. Anna, Sally, and Lorraine sing "Here we are together all sitting on the rug." Each line is a different child's name; the children clown around and each falls down laughing when his or her name is sung. They sing, "Mary Mack" and four children do hand motions with the song. The chorus is, "Hio, hio, hio, Ohio." Bluejay sings out in unison, and it is suddenly clear that all morning Bluejay's funny rhythmic babbling had really been this song. They sing, "Open Shut Them" and "Ring Around the Rosey," both to excited squeals at the familiar surprising endings.

"Routine includes all the people, material, and events that kids can expect in the course of the day," Anna says later. "You could argue that these kids are a little young for Circle, but it gives them a sense of control and security to know what's coming. They know what they can count on, and that's calming and strengthening for them."

"After lunch Bluejay goes to his bed," Sally adds. "He can predict what's next, and that makes him feel safe and good. It's also important for us to know we're moving along. You don't want to be rigid, but sometimes it's a relief to know that lunch is coming and then nap."

After lunch Anna reads *Ten, Nine, Eight* by Molly Bang, while Sally and Lorraine get beds ready for nap. "Ten small toes all washed and warm. . . ." The bedtime countdown begins and there is a picture of the little girl's brown toes on a bright red rug. "Five round buttons on a yellow gown. . . ." The beautiful little girl sits on her father's lap in her cuddly nightshirt. "One big girl all ready for bed. . . ." She is tucked under her quilt holding her fuzzy bear and looking out with quiet eyes.

Eliot and Max are already asleep and are carried to their beds. Anna lies down near Asha and pats her back; Sally is rocking Alessia in her arms; and Lorraine is rubbing Zach's head. Slowly, trustingly, they all drift off to sleep.

Anna's 94-year-old grandmother recently moved from Cuba to New York, where Anna and her mother can care for her more easily. "She's very alert," says Anna, "but a lot of work. She misses her 90-year-old sister and misses feeding the chickens and sitting with her dog. She also hates the elevators, and each trip out is a major struggle because she's on the eighteenth floor." But Anna is also glad for the chance to be with her grandmother at this time. "She took care of us and now we will take care of her. The never-ending circle of love has no beginning and has no ending."

## ☆ 3 ☆

# CHANA
# Balance and Loss

Chana Stein is a group family day-care provider in New York City. She began taking children into her home while she was caring for her own two children and has continued that work even though her youngest son began elementary school six years ago. Chana cares for 12 children, and she and her staff have an elaborate program of activities, trips, and events every day. Hers is an exemplary day-care home, and she is often asked to speak about day-care issues at community and professional gatherings. Chana has a master's degree from Bank Street College of Education in New York City, and she is a leader in the effort to obtain some form of official recognition for group family day care.

While most other industrialized nations provide comprehensive support for child care, the United States does not. A 1971 bill providing for a nationwide system of child-care centers based on ability to pay passed both houses of Congress but was vetoed by President Nixon, who commented on the importance of women staying in the home. The United States is alone among Western industrialized nations in failing to calculate the need for child care or to identify what child-care arrangements exist.

Most experts estimate that over six million children spend ten or more hours in some form of group family day care, that is, in the home of a baby-sitter, a neighbor, or a relative. This is sketchy, in part because the situation for families and children is changing so rapidly that any estimate is also instantly obsolete. Furthermore, almost 90 percent of family day care is unlicensed, unregulated, and underground. Day care is scattered, and our understanding of it is vague.

It is certain that the range of what constitutes group family day care is vast. I've been in homes where the smell of sour milk and soiled diapers is intense, and the wail of the television competes with the bawling of unattended babies. But I've also been in day-care homes where the rhythms of family life are recreated in imaginative and caring ways. I'm sure that between these extremes exists every possible variation. I'm also certain that this ancient form of child care is widespread and growing, and should be better understood and attended to.

Chana is a group family day-care provider. "Don't call me a teacher," she insists. "I run a group family day-care home. People who say they 'teach' kids eighteen months to four years old are doing something I don't do. I don't have a credential and I don't identify with it. I could teach, and, believe me, life would be easier, but then I would have abandoned something I've fought for for years." I continue to use the word "teacher" occasionally, but I mean it in the broadest sense of someone who engages whole people—mind, body, emotion, culture, spirit—in learning. But each time I say "teacher" in her presence, I am immediately corrected.

"I was born in Philadelphia," Chana says, "and raised in a Jewish neighborhood after the war. It was a striving, middle-class environment with clean, new schools. Everyone I saw was rising together, and everyone I knew was very much alike. By junior high school and high school there were some non-Jewish kids in the group, but there were always so many of us and we were the smartest and belonged to all the clubs, that I never felt outside of anything. I can see the problems and limitations of that life now, but it was at that time a safe harbor for me—a place from which to grow up with confidence and feeling."

Characteristically, as soon as Chana reads her transcribed comments, her objections begin. "I guess I am uncomfortable with the beginning of this portrait because we devote so few words to a whole community's experiences. It makes my view seem trivial." She is a substantial woman, combining elements in equal measure that would seem contradictory in another person: She is opinionated and open, caring and demanding, understanding and convinced. She is also self-assured, dependable, and unequivocal. "I am not wispy. I am not airy," she says by way of self-description. "I met a Torah scribe recently who told about his craft and taught calligraphy to teachers in Jewish schools. Many of us did not have Hebrew names—especially those of us born before Israel existed. We came from a shtetl tradition with Yiddish names. I was asked for my name in preparing forms for my son Josh's Bar Mitzvah. The Torah scribe had a list and told me Chana Matanah is my Hebrew name. I like it." Chana Matanah means gift, and she is a solid and undivided gift, as you will see.

Chana and her sister were raised in an old-fashioned extended family. Her mother started working during World War II, and her father was often away on business. "In a sense my grandmother raised me, and she was a wonderful mother. On top of that, I had an aunt who looked exactly like my mother (her identical twin), and her husband, and my mother's brother—and all of us living under one roof." It was a nurturing set of people for a child to have, and that felt good. "The daily separations from my mother were so early in my life and so natural that I'm not sure we felt them as separations at all. We all lived together, and lots of people were in charge of me. I wasn't bundled and dropped. No vital toys or bottles were left behind. All objects stayed the same. No guilt. No conflicts that I can remember. When we moved to our own house, the first thing I learned to do was to take the bus to grandma's. My grandfather was ill and a shut-in, and I spent my weekends with them." Her most powerful early memories involve time with her grandfather—making ice cream in a freezing tray, drinking tea with lots of milk and sugar, collecting pictures of automobiles from magazines and the faces of movie stars that came as a promotion in the bread they bought—and her grandmother—singing Russian songs, organizing efforts for the International Ladies Garment Workers Union (ILGWU), helping to sort her piecework and collect tickets for "a partial," the partial unemployment benefits available to part-time workers.

Chana's parents started a small accounting firm, and her mother had an office in the house. But there is a small crack in the almost perfect picture just described. Chana remembers her sister and herself complaining about the family business because there was a sense of their mother being divided and preoccupied. There was often something to do in the office, and their mother would go there after dinner or on Sundays. There were clients coming and going in the evenings. Chana says now that she and her sister grew up respecting their parents' involvement in the community, but it was an involvement that sometimes drew their parents away, and so they had a typical childlike complaint: "We thought if she had a regular job then when she was home she would be completely there for us. It's a laugh to me now, because I sometimes think my own kids experience a similar problem with my work. Their space is so completely invaded by my work, and I'm always at home and at work simultaneously. I think they must sometimes think that if I had a real job at least I could call in sick or take vacation once in a while."

Her apartment is not only home for her, her husband, and their two sons, it is also the home-away-from-home for seventeen toddlers who attend on a complex staggered schedule. The apartment reflects both realities: a large and comfortable home with a lovely old breakfront, a grand piano, crowded bookshelves, and walls adorned with paintings, pictures, and family photographs, including ancient relatives and cousins in Israel; and a well-organized day-care center with changing table and potty chairs, step stools and booster seats, art materials and manipulatives. Except for Chana's bedroom, which is off-limits and behind the only closed door in the apartment, the entire space flip-flops everyday and serves two complementary but very different needs. On one visit her younger son, Daniel, was home from school with the flu, and so he was in his parents' room. He slept and read and played quietly. Daniel, eight years old, had been part of the day care as a toddler himself and now seems to take the constraints of the toddler invasion in stride: "I keep my stuff put away and it's not a big deal. If there's a big mess I don't like it, but it's usually okay."

The building is solid, the lobby spacious and clean, with mirrors and ornamental tiles, the elevators speedy and efficient. It is not difficult to find Chana's apartment on the sixth floor; the visitor simply follows the sounds of children's voices and laughter and tears around a corner and down to the end of a corridor where there is a parking lot of carriages and strollers. "The neighbors put up with a lot," Chana admits sympathetically. "And they say encouraging things to me all the time. The building and the neighborhood are traditionally German-Jewish. There are many older people. They seem to like the kids," she says.

On the door to apartment 6C is a cardboard sign with a plastic cylinder taped to it and in large letters a message: "No-choke testing tube—a simple test for safety—$1.00." Next to the sign is a clipboard with a note saying, "We are going to the nursing home this morning." Inside the door is a closet and a short corridor leading to the dining room. Along the length of the corridor is a bulletin board for parents, and directly below and parallel to it is a long mirror at knee level (eye level for toddlers). The bulletin board is busy with information for parents: an article entitled "12 Alternatives to Whacking Your Kid," a list of neighborhood social services, a pamphlet called "What You Can Do to Stop Disease in Your Child's Day-Care Center," an envelope of voter registration forms, a xeroxed page with a large heading "HEAD LICE," an information sheet about library programs, an advertisement for automobile restraints, a pamphlet about a parenting center run out of the "Y," an article about reading to your young child, a notice about children's television, and an envelope of notes concerning frequent activities or announcements for use, when appropriate, on the front door, for example, "We are planting today," "Painting with Florence," "In the playground," "Movement today with Joanne Brown," "Welcome back," "We need paper," "Music today with Toby."

Opposite the mirror and down into the dining room a bit is a low, long set of pegs for coats and hats. Under each peg rests a cardboard square for boots or shoes, with a set of silhouetted feet cut from colorful, patterned paper, and a child's name pasted to each. The dining room table is covered with plastic, on top of which is a pile of construction paper, some magic markers, several rolls of brightly colored tape, and three varieties of age-appropriate scissors: the classic small, dull round-nosed type; a space-age spring-action set to be gripped as if shaking hands; and an ingenious pair with small finger holes for a young child snuggled beneath large finger holes for an adult hand.

"Oh, it's hard to wait," Chana empathizes with Oren, who is spinning anxiously in his seat while another child chooses which tape to use. Two children are working busily, seated on booster chairs. Oren, who doesn't want a booster, is shifting this way and that in the grown-up dining room chair. "Here, Oren, it's your turn. I'm going to turn you around so you're more comfortable. If you don't want a booster then move around here on your knees so you can reach the table." Oren begins to cut tape and stick it gleefully to the paper.

The dining room is the central room; off of it are a den, the kitchen, the living room, and a corridor leading to the bathroom and the bedrooms. The den is a beehive of early childhood energy and purpose. Iliusha is working on a puzzle with great animation. He is large and loud, and he exclaims as he fits each piece together with bursts of heart and spit, and great dramatic gestures accompanied by powerful Russian phrases. Two children are going on a make-believe shopping trip with little red and yellow plastic shopping carts piled with dolls and stuffed animals. One child has a hat on and a jangling row of bracelets up one arm. "We're going to the supermarket," she says. "I'm the super-mommy and you're the super-daddy."

In the kitchen Joann, one of Chana's assistants, oversees the making of apple crisp for a special snack. Three children on booster chairs have been pulled up to the long kitchen table and are using dull plastic knives, cutting apples like mad into all imaginable shapes and sizes from massive chunks to tiny slivers. A lot of apple makes it into a large mixing bowl, and a lot is eaten by the cooks themselves. As she works alongside the children, Joann talks about the recipe and how they will proceed. She doesn't mind their eating, but she reminds the children several times not to put the knives into their mouths. "Serious cooks don't put knives in their mouths." The children nod and chop and chew.

The bell sounds, and Joann answers the intercom and then buzzes in a new arrival. In a few minutes Gina bursts through the door followed by her mother. Gina is two, bundled in coat and scarf and hat, with just a bit of round face and sparkling eyes peeking out. Chana greets them and kneels down alongside to chat as Gina's mother unbundles her, revealing a sturdy, smiling girl. After a trip to the bathroom and some last-minute instructions, Gina's mother is ready to leave. Chana lifts Gina up for a last hug and then tries to interest her in an activity in the den. Gina is comfortable in Chana's arms, her body and face relaxed; she insists, "One more hug," and Chana easily agrees. Gina suggests they walk Mommy to the door, and they do. Chana proposes they go in now, but Gina wants to walk Mommy to the elevator. Chana goes along and they say good-bye again. Chana now asks, "Do you want to wave from the window?" and Gina does. So they wait a minute and then open the hall window and Gina stands on the sill holding onto the child-protection grate and yells good-bye. "This is the ritual of the window," Chana explains, smiling. "The kids love it, and I only worry about the neighbors when the kids dance on the radiator and make too much noise." From six floors below, Gina's mother waves and blows kisses, and Gina laughs and jumps down, heading eagerly back to Chana.

Just as Gina joins the cooking crew, Carol arrives. She comes only two mornings a week, and she is not really settled in on this day when her mother hurries off. Chana holds her and rocks her but she sobs and sobs. "I want Mommy." Soon her face is puffy and red and dripping. Chana, wiping nose and eyes, rocks her and softly chants a kind of soothing mantra: "Mommies go away, and mommies come back; mommies go away, and mommies come back." The sobbing recedes a bit, and then returns full force. "I want her, I want her." Chana comforts and affirms. "You want your Mommy," she says softly. "Mommy will come back after lunch. Mommy's working."

"No, she's not working."

"Well, she's working on something. Remember she told you she'd be back after lunch and she told me to take good care of you and to check your Pamper and to put Desitin on your rash? Let's check it now."

[Later, when reading this section, Chana commented, "It's all true, but me? A mantra? Cute."]

After a time Chana moves into the den and pulls a large shoe box from a shelf. In it are well-handled contact-covered photographs of mothers and fathers, grandmothers and grandfathers, dogs and friends and vacations, and happy day-care moments like trips to the playground and the nursing home. She finds Carol's pictures and they look at them together. A couple of other children clamber onto the couch and sort through the pictures, finding their own photographs. Soon photographs are strewn in all directions, and Carol has found one that she clutches tightly to her stomach.

Chana moves Carol off her lap for the first time and gets down an audio tape from another shelf and puts it in the tape player. The tape is Carol's mother reading a favorite book. Carol listens for a time and then cries a bit more. "I can't hear," Sarah complains. "Well," Chana responds gently, "she's having a personal cry, and it's hard for her to do it quietly."

Chana lies on her side on the floor with a box of small letter blocks. "Which block would Mommy like?"

"She likes both," Carol says seriously. It is a first authentic response, a real answer, engaged and thoughtful. Chana sets her to building a pile of blocks that Mommy would like. She works methodically, but she is still low-keyed and without enthusiasm. Her language begins to blossom some: "I need this one. I like this." But she is not yet fully herself.

"Separation is the curriculum," Chana explains later. "It's the whole program. And I think it's the central issue in child care. I'm very explicit about it with parents and with other providers. When parents come and see my home, it looks like such a wonderful place to visit, so many interesting things for kids to do, so inviting. Parents who are anxious about academics, see the letterboard, for example, right away, even though I think it's stuck way off in the other room. They see the preschool experience that they think will get their kid ready to read. But I'm very clear. I'm not promising anything. They're not going to read; they probably won't know their letters by the time they leave me. 'But she's so bright!'

They're all bright. Fine. All I commit to, and what I work on, is that children will feel okay here without their parents, that they'll be able to acknowledge the difficulties and still participate fully in life here. That's the whole program."

Chana's thinking about separation and about her engagement with kids and families around the issue of separation is a classic example of a teacher at work. When Chana interviews parents, she describes why separation is such a critical issue for young children. She discusses the tension between connectedness and autonomy, and she gives them materials to read. "We expect more than a change of clothes from parents," Chana says. "We want people to be prepared to spend enough time here in the beginning to allow the child to feel comfortable, we want photographs and tapes from home, we want to create a comfortable bridge for kids. We do home visits and we do small groups of kids visiting each home during the year. Of course, people interpret it differently. Some people do it in the way we had hoped they would; others say, 'But I have to be some place at 10 o'clock and I hope my kid isn't one who needs more time!' We have to live with that. There's bound to be a tension between what would be ideal and the realities of people's lives. Anyone getting one of the slots in our program is very fortunate, and anyone who can spend the kind of time we would like working on separation until it is really comfortable for everyone is certainly privileged."

The audio tapes of parents and grandparents talking and reading favorite stories is inventive. There are two tape players, and children can listen in two rooms. 'It's something I had done with my own kids," Chana explains, "but in a different way. My in-laws live far away and so I asked them to make tapes for my kids. I saw that it was somehow very meaningful to them, somehow a meaningful connection, even to laugh at Grandpa's accent, at his mispronunciations. My kids know 'Frog and Toad' backwards and forwards, and when Grandpa says 'Frog and Todd' we can listen and laugh and also have a pleasant memory. I also miss my own grandfather, and when I recommend that parents tape grandparents reading and talking, I think about what a treasure it will be."

Chana first used tapes in her teaching when she began to get children whose first language was not English. These children were having the same separation difficulties as everyone else, but these difficulties were compounded by the children's being unable to communicate in English with some important adults. "I asked these parents for tapes, and I got 'The Carrot Seed' in Nepali and 'Goodnight Moon' in Serbo-Croatian, and I thought, 'This is great!' They were a comfort. It was an easy step from there to using that with all kids."

There are a lot of nonworking telephones for the children, and they play a lot at calling mommy and telling her what they need. "Kids use them because their parents use them; the telephone is a very meaningful instrument in today's life," Chana explains. "We also tell parents who can't stay in the beginning to go out for an hour and then call to check in. When they call, if all is well they're so relieved and they don't want to talk because that could be upsetting. I usually say, 'Look, if it's upsetting, let's let her get it out. Why should she have to hold herself together?' I mean it's like the parents who try to distract the kid in the morning and then sneak out. I'm against that. I think you need honest, reliable messages, and you need to allow for some honest upset. Some people are very much afraid of that crying. I think I'm pretty good at suffering the sadness and the letdown of separation, and then really enjoying the reunion—perhaps because my early separations weren't dreadful for me and I learned in my own extended family to trust separation. In any case I'm not torn up about separation questions and in a sense that makes me the perfect person for what I do."

Later I asked Chana to describe a powerful memory of separation.

"I can't seem to get an organized answer to your question about separation," she wrote. "I guess I am focusing narrowly on school separation issues, and because of the times I didn't have a school experience until attending a half-day kindergarten. Given what I see babies experience and endure—in my own home—it seems ridiculous to make any comparison. I really don't remember with any passion that experience."

After a while she went on. "The real separations of my life were the death of my grandfather and my aunt Sylvia, my mother's twin sister. Since I was eleven at the first and in my late twenties at the second, it seems odd to relate them to my work. In some ways they were separations well prepared for by wasting illness and some sense of acknowledgment of the situation, which I believe is critical to the successful resolution or integration of the experience."

Chana's grandfather was housebound, then bound to one floor, one room, and one chair. "As his world constricted, the TV, radio, telephone, and newspapers became his connectors. I always thought he was the smartest man in the world. Now as I am writing I realize that he was no intellectual. He never had books brought in, didn't subscribe to magazines, and didn't express deep political commitments. Yet he seemed to me to be bright, exciting, interested in everything. He was interested in me, which is what makes me cry when I let myself remember him. He was sure I was the best—and so proud. His support was uncomplicated. His agenda was to spend as much time together as possible—and to enjoy it all we could. I think we watched baseball on TV. I am sure we heard the games on the radio. We listened to all the old-time radio stories—Suspense, Johnny Dollar, Henry Aldrich, Beulah, Amos and Andy. We listened to news and watched Dave Garroway. We discussed everything we saw. We ate candy and peanuts from a can, and ice cream."

In a way this memory makes Chana feel sorry for her own children. "We are all so busy that no one is just for them—absolutely delighted in teaching and listening to them. Since grandparents are all at a distance and quite modern, we are fortunate to have found our equivalent—a paid tutor. She is a wonderfully eclectic woman who exudes love and warmth. She is a demanding teacher with high standards and enormous insight. She sees each of our boys weekly and consults with us frequently. She is unlike anyone else we know. In some ways the full and complete attention to the children and the closed but enriched atmosphere in her home remind me of my grandfather. How interesting that I remember hours on end of this, and today we scratch to find one hour per week! Could more be tolerated? Is my memory a distortion?"

The death of Chana's aunt, although not as protracted in length, had a similar pattern of gradually restricted activity. She was the person who introduced Chana to traveling around Philadelphia. She was the outside agent of experiences, as her grandfather had been the inside one.

Chana's aunt had been ill with cancer for about two years before her death. During that time she had a few short periods of remission. When Chana realized that her aunt would die soon, she returned to Philadelphia to her parents' home and to her dying aunt.

"A few days after I arrived home, she was rushed to the hospital," Chana writes, "where little could be done but make her comfortable. She was put in a large storage room. I stayed in her room every night for the two weeks she lived. At first we had long discussions that were continuations of all the previous discussions in our lives. It was a summing-up. She wanted me to know her present position on all issues. She commented on my personal life, although uninvited. Eventually she couldn't talk, only point and move her face. We found a way to communicate with pats and comforting looks. She died on a Sunday morning. Her brother had come to visit and to relieve me. She seemed quite alert (more so than she had been for several days). Somehow we all agreed that I should stay longer. He left. She relaxed. She shook and coughed and choked and died." Chana says she doesn't usually cry when she remembers her aunt. "She didn't exactly tell everyone that she knew she was dying, but she left everyone with a plan or a message for their future without her. She acknowledged a change was happening. I think today she would have called a family meeting or at least had even more direct, open acknowledgment from everyone."

Chana says, "I am not sure if this experience is really related to children's daily separations from their parents in my home. It is good child development practice to acknowledge the pain and loss of separation for both sides. We do that here easily and naturally. We use pictures, tapes, and telephone calls to help parent and child through the experience. Events of the day and photos are posted on the front door—to prepare, build links, remember, remind. The literature is there. Perhaps we reflect our own experiences in the special commitment we give to whatever part of good practice we really feel. In this sense, I feel well prepared to share in easing separations. I am comfortable with tears, special transitional objects, and talking about anger and loss. This program is not a one-person show. If the other staff people do not share this commitment, it won't work. Since I don't know their experiences of separation, I believe they commit to this way because it works and I am the boss."

Of other separations in her life, Chana says, "My move to New York, my ending 9-to-5 downtown employment, and my sister's move to Israel are all important, but none of these is as final and unchangeable as death. None was as well prepared for as the two deaths I have experienced, although my sister's move came close. In some ways the main difference is that acceptance is not enough. Some new adjusted relationship must continue. The fun is in the details of the adjustment. Those situations must also have some bearing on how I see what the kids and parents are experiencing."

While one of the other care givers finishes cleaning up, Chana and Joann begin to change, toilet, and bundle up a group of children for the trip to the nursing home. They work steadily and purposefully, describing the trip, reminding kids of their visit last week, solving crises, and overcoming obstacles; in 20 minutes the parade of double strollers and care givers and hand-holding walkers head out the door. In the elevator Carol remembers her mother and begins again to cry softly, "I want Mommy."

In the lobby several older people smile and nod, a few bend down to kooch the children in high-pitched, sing-song voices. One woman asks Chana if she knows anyone who might be available to clean in her daughter's new kosher restaurant. Chana says she will keep it in mind and has her own request: "We're trying to collect blood for Harriet Eisner. She's at Einstein Hospital and needs B-negative. If you know anyone who can help, please call me."

On the street, people smile, wave, and speak. One woman tells Chana she found a store in the neighborhood to get "sensible shoes," and Chana thanks her. The nursing home is around the corner and so, for all the preparation and bundling up, the group arrives in four minutes. Through the front doors the social worker, a middle-aged woman with large glasses and the traditional wig and hat of an orthodox Jew, greets the children with genuine enthusiasm. She speaks to each by name and helps unbundle them and put their things on a couch in her office, on one wall of which are eight photographs of previous visits—children and old people sharing a snack, a conversation, or a song—with a large heading: "Chana's Toddler Care and Us." This relationship appears to have a mutual benefit and a shared importance.

The children know the way to the recreation area, and several rush down a corridor, through swinging double doors, past a waiting area with a forlorn traffic jam of wheelchairs and immobilized people waiting, and into the room with a table set up for them. Nine ancient women in wheelchairs are pulled up to the table as the children swirl in: Jesse is sleeping with her head tilted back; Lillian laughs and claps as the children arrive; Aileen begins talking to Daniel, who smiles every few words and says "No" without deterring Aileen in the least; Esther takes a child's hand and pats it lovingly. Chana greets the old women by name, going from one to the other, touching each on the arm or the hand, asking about family. Fanny, regal but emaciated, looks up at her through thick bifocals and flashes yellow teeth through a worried smile. Chana introduces herself to Ethel, and Alexandra says, "She's new."

"What's new?" responds Ethel. "I'm old."

"Never mind," says Alexandra. "I'm here two years. It's okay. What are you going to do?"

Everyone shares a laugh.

The nursing-home and toddler-care staffs serve a snack of apples and oranges, toast with marmalade, and juice to the old and young people gathered around the table. As they eat, the staffs sing a name song called "Here We Are Together" in which each name is sung in turn. Several clap in time or sing bits of the song. After snack everyone shares paper and markers to make pictures together for one of the children's birthdays. Aileen encourages Daniel to keep the markers neat and in order, saying, "Keep it nice and together and they won't get lost." Daniel smiles as he works furiously on the paper, oblivious to her well-meaning advice. Carol remembers her mother again, and Chana picks her up, explaining to general sympathy that she is having a rough day missing her mother.

For this group in their unique dialogue and their joyful joint projects, the antiseptic smell and the hospital equipment fade into the background and are replaced by the happiness of mutual caring. For these few mo-

ments Chana has created an extended family of the very young and the
very old, the vital and the infirm—a reflection of a long-ago memory.

Chana accepts this description of time in the nursing home, but is not
so sure about the "reflection of a long-ago memory." She comments that
often she has a hard time getting herself to go there because "the group
gets me down." She is also disturbed by the lack of a first-rate staff, the
obvious compromises in care, and the "politics" of the nursing home.

When asked at another time to create a metaphor for working with
young children, Chana wrote that working with young children is like
marriage. "Both are full of stresses and tensions. Being successful, while
socially approved, is undervalued, misunderstood, and unexamined.
Both can be warm and including, or lonely and excluding, can hold you
together or pull you apart. Both are exhausting and exhilarating. Both
can be a refuge and a prison."

Family is obviously important to Chana, a central theme and metaphor
that emerges and re-emerges. It is where she finds purpose and meaning.
She is rooted in it and propelled by it. Her sense of family, while central,
is neither sentimentalized nor sanitized. "I keep a kosher home but it's
my own standard of kosher. We eat pizza. We have a regular Saturday.
We're involved in a synagogue that reaches out and takes care of more
than its own. We're together Friday night. The kids like that ritual, but
me, I'm tired."

She sees family-building as intense, difficult work. "None of these relationships is easy or natural or obvious," she says. "Becoming a parent
was an enormous adjustment for me, very difficult and unpleasant in lots
of ways. Josh was born by Caesarian and that was a shock. I was prepared
for natural childbirth and unprepared for a Caesarian. I felt I'd done
something wrong. I had failed. And physically, too, I was wiped out. Also,
I'd been a big deal as a social worker for 12 years. I could shake things
up. And here I couldn't stop this infant from crying sometimes, and the
cry was electrifying to me. I was exhausted and I felt incompetent—all
the skills I had and felt so good about were completely irrelevant. My
husband was a great shock, because while he's probably more supportive
than most fathers, somehow he wasn't up to my standard. I mean he went
to work that first week, and my whole life had just crashed. He'd say that
he had to go, but did he? Things I'd never done before became my job,
housewife things, things like going to the cleaners and the post office. I
got lots of advice from neighbors about how to take care of my baby, good-
spirited advice but not always welcome. I still get advice in the hallway
and on the street, but it doesn't get to me now."

When Josh was eighteen months old, Chana got together seven other women and formed a baby-sitting co-op. She described that network as a life raft. "Now I'm a life raft for other families, something people need, something I really needed myself."

Chana's academic orientation combined with her strong self-reliance told her that any problem could be read about, studied, and understood. She took a weekend course in parenting issues at Bank Street College, and when Josh was two, she enrolled him in a day-care center near Bank Street and started school full-time. She worked at the day-care center one day a week, but the arrangement didn't work out. Chana felt instinctively that the teacher wasn't really doing what needed to be done for two-year-olds, nor was she doing what Chana was learning in her classes at Bank Street. For example, Josh was out of diapers, and the teacher wanted him to pee at specific convenient times, like before going to the park; and he couldn't always accommodate. And Josh tended to fall asleep a little later than most children ("nap is a critical separation time"), and she couldn't adjust to his need to sleep a little later. The teacher woke all the children up at a certain time, no matter what. Chana traces to this difficult time for Josh her own decision to keep one room open and free of sleepers during nap time, so that those who wake up early can play while those who need to can continue to sleep. In any case, the situation at the day-care center continued to deteriorate.

"One day," Chana recalls, "the teacher called me at my student teaching placement, and I could hear Josh shrieking in the background. She said, 'You talk to him.' I couldn't believe it. Here was my little boy going to pieces, and he was the whole reason for my becoming a perfect parent to the point of getting a degree in it. And the teacher actually expected me to deal with him over the phone. I was terribly upset."

The situation became tense and more difficult. Relations were strained. One day the teacher told Chana she was unhappy that Josh didn't hold hands during "Ring Around the Rosey." Chana said she couldn't think of a time when she'd made a circle with the grown-ups all around her and she thought Josh would be okay anyway. "I was hostile and things weren't going well. She was furious. 'Then you take responsibility for his social development' she commanded. I said, 'What are you talking about? I already take responsibility for his every development. I'm the mommy here. Let's not confuse who's who.'"

Josh got sick soon after that, and Chana's husband took off from work because she had to be at her student teaching placement. "This became an issue for me because here I was being worked to death and getting no pay, and I couldn't even be home with my sick kid. I'm stumbling up the steps to my placement leaving my own kid home sick. Absurd! This is in my mind now as I try to do things completely differently. People are paying me to have enough people here and to have a substitute when I need one. I want my center to be nurturing to the providers and their children as well as to the families we serve. How can we give to others if we're being drained ourselves?"

When Chana's second child, Daniel, was two she decided to start a play group in her own home. She felt more relaxed about parenting, and had built some confidence at Bank Street and some prestige from the baby-sitting co-op. She was interested and competent. She was in a women's group, and when she said that she didn't want to go back to work or school and described what she had in mind, people were supportive. One woman said, "If you do that I'm sending you my kid!" So it began.

Chana told her parents about her project, and they sent her an unsupportive letter with a fictitious help-wanted ad for a mother for her own children, along with a check to entice her to abandon her plan. "I was furious," Chana remembers. "I shared that letter with my women's group. I kept the money and went ahead with the project."

When Chana later read a draft of this portrait she wrote:

"When I read this I was shaken. I realize that I left out many things in our brief discussions that would provide a more rounded picture. Although my parents were reluctant at first to see me begin child care, they have been supportive. For several years they have taken one or both kids during their extra winter vacations so that I don't have to work with both of them underfoot. I have been disappointed in my parents in a way. I always thought grandparents were supposed to be relaxed and accepting and forgiving. My parents have managed to maintain their same standards, and sometimes the kids can't breathe in their presence. But there's also a whole body of things we agree about, and they can be very generous. My mother is my accountant. She suffered with my poor record keeping until I had a trusted assistant take over. She trained the assistant and set up simple books for us. She has always suggested money-saving techniques and never questioned the staff costs. She reads family day-care record-keeping material and looks for articles about financing child care. She sends every article about family day care that appears in the Philadelphia papers, and she sends 'care packages.'"

The first year was an informal, four-days-a-week, pay-when-you-come affair. Very quickly Chana realized she didn't want to be alone, and so she hired a person to work with her. Chana's best memory of that year was having Daniel with her. There was never a question about what to do, because she was being Daniel's mother and the other children were part of their lives. "That year we did Chanukah and not Christmas, and we went to a sukkah because it was right here in the building. When Daniel moved on, the question of not imposing on others became more important. I think I liked it best as a home extension. But there's a natural pull to being a professional center for children, especially when my own kids left."

Chana was part of a network called the Infant-Toddler Twos Network when she learned about another network at the "Y" that trained family day-care providers and helped them with licensing. She contacted them. Prior to that she had not known that there was a license for family care, but felt that if there were some official certificate to get, then she needed to get it. "The regulation required that there be one care giver for five children," Chana says, "and I thought I'd be in great shape because I have an enormous apartment and I had eight kids and two care givers. This is better. Well, I was wrong. By the time the Health Department came, we had twelve kids and three care givers. We wanted them to see how wonderful we were, how we let the kids pass the food and pour their own juice at lunch, how kids were developing with us; but the worker came and checked forms and measured floors. She missed all the most important things. It was deflating. When she saw how many kids were here, she said she'd have to write for an exception to policy. Okay. I fully expected to get an exception because I so clearly had an exceptionally fine program. It was clear. Months later I got a certificate allowing me to have five children here. It's a joke; I never even hung it up. I've been out of compliance from the first day, and I've been fighting almost as long for some official recognition for group family day care."

Chana feels the injustice of the situation strongly. "None of the rules or regulations recognize that this is a family occupation, that it happens where people live, and that it has the potential to be a safer, more stimulating, and better experience for children. They would permit me to be alone in the apartment with five kids, and because of racist quirks in the law I could even have six kids if I were subsidized by the Agency for Child Development. The Health Department doesn't have anyone to come out and check on me; they only respond to complaints. And yet group family care is outside the law. It's crazy."

After years of struggle a state law was passed creating a pilot project for group family care, and although Chana was one of the leaders of the effort, she didn't qualify for the pilot because her apartment is not on the first floor. The pilot permitted twelve children to two care givers on the first floor. "All over New York there are six kids to one care giver on any floor at all," Chana complains, "but here I am with twelve and three and I can't qualify. My situation is better, but they don't have any way to see or understand that."

The law establishing the category of group family day care was signed by Governor Cuomo in August 1986, largely through the efforts of Chana and the people she has brought together. "We're waiting for the Department of Social Services to issue guidelines, but for me, I remain illegal. I think they know this is a quality program, and they'd just as soon ignore us as long as there's no formal complaint. If I abandoned the idea of group family care I could do a lot, but I just can't give it up, can't give in to the stupidity. I'm more interested in the professionally unaccredited people who do this work than I am in the abstract question of professionalism. Sometimes I ask myself, 'All of this for 12 kids?' It's a mood I get into. Other times I say 'If I were the Commissioner of Something I could change the world.' I get stuck between the poles."

Chana is deeply involved in political and community groups. She describes her involvements as a dilemma or a delicate balance, because they bring her into the world of other professionals, peers, and community activists, which pulls her away from her work even as it allows her to do her work. It gives her energy and it drains her energy. "I couldn't do the kids full time," she says. "Even though time away is about the kids, I find it renewing. If I'm away too much, then being with the kids is restorative. Ironically, I think this whole political involvement and sense of community service is very much a reflection of my parents' values. My father was always lending someone money, helping a family bail someone out of jail, assisting someone in the hospital. There are echoes of that here."

Chana reflects on the future: "In five years, who knows what I'll be doing? The physical challenge of this can be too much. I've thought about law, but you have to put up with a lot of nonsense in law too. Whatever I do I want it to be meaningful, humane, and important. I want to be in charge of my own schedule. I got into this because of my kids, and the kids pull in new directions. They've moved on and I probably will too."

When Chana read this, she wrote:

"I am distressed about my having to struggle to write my thoughts and reactions to what you have written. I am sure you understand that there are multiple and complex reasons (excuses?)—and too many challenges for the hours in a day—every day. In addition, the process of self-examination, stepping out of the rush and watching, is very jarring. This isn't a narrow section of life but touches everything. It is overwhelming for me to realize how this group family day-care advocacy effort has become a bridge to the rest of the world for me. In a sense, it has been an organizing principle that helps me set priorities, make family decisions, and keep moving when I might want to stop. It seems that the advocacy effort has almost become the work—with the staff and children and program commitments the afterthought. Some of your questions about the work made me realize that I have to make (or have been making) decisions that might lead me away from it or back into it. I don't know which."

Chana wrote in January, about a year after our last conversation: "We are okay. The day care is closing on June 10. I'm sad and relieved, still a bit ambivalent, you see, but I had to decide now so that parents could find other arrangements. Now that the decision is final, I can begin to consider my alternatives."

# ☆ 4 ☆

# JOANNE
## To Make a Difference

JoAnne Williams has worked in day care for over 10 years as founder, director, and now collective member of JoAnne's Day Care Community in New York City. JoAnne is largely self-educated, having read widely and deeply in child development and early childhood education. The fact that she never attended college surprises colleagues and associates because of her broad knowledge of and huge reputation in the field. She often speaks at early childhood conferences, and she was profiled recently in a national magazine for developing an exemplary nonsexist and nonracist program.

Because day care is expensive, hard to find, and difficult to manage, many working mothers arrange a kind of crazy quilt of care for their children. A child, for example, may be left at a baby-sitter early so that a mother can get to work, may spend half a day in Head Start or a play group, and may be picked up and brought home by a grandmother or a family friend. This patching together of bits and pieces to make an entire day, a pattern that is typical for many families, explains in part why it is so hard to get a firm hold on what kind of child care exists.

There are over a million children in organized, licensed day-care centers in this country. Head Start, for all its popularity, serves fewer than half a million children, only 18 percent of those eligible. Kindercare, the large commercial child-care chain, claims to have 800 centers. Four hundred hospitals and two hundred other businesses (out of six million employers) provide some form of on-site child care.

The range of care in all these settings is enormous. Some centers are highly institutional, with children moving as a group on a fixed schedule from playpens to high chairs to potties to naps; other centers are places where children are cherished as unique individuals and develop close and warm relationships with caring adults who nurture them as well as stimulate them to discover, to achieve, and to grow.

It's early morning and JoAnne is sitting on the floor sorting through photographs, posters, drawings, and magazines. "Oh, look at this one, Caitlin!" she exclaims, holding up a striking poster of four muscular women dancing in a circle, colorful scarves held high as a flock of flamingoes soar off into the purple burning sky. "Ooh!" says Caitlin. "That's beautiful. Let's put it here." She points to the center of the bulletin board.

"Maybe," says JoAnne. "But let's see everything we have first and then decide what goes where."

Caitlin is five years old now, a recent day-care graduate. Today is a public school holiday, and JoAnne has invited her to spend the day as an "assistant teacher" at the day-care center. Caitlin seems delighted to see old friends as the other children arrive, and quite comfortable to be back in the place that had been her second home from the time she was 10 months old until she went off to kindergarten.

Caitlin is sorting through a large file folder marked "Women's History."

Two other folders lean against the wall, and posters are strewn about in emerging stacks. "JoAnne, look!" Caitlin cries. She holds up a picture of Zaida Gonzales, one of the first women to break into the ranks of the New York City Fire Department, in full fire-fighter regalia. "Oh, good," says JoAnne enthusiastically. "I knew we had that somewhere. Put it in this pile here." Caitlin places it carefully in a pile and returns to rifling through the folder. "Now I want to find the one of me in the fire hat," she says.

Caitlin is referring to a picture from a trip last year to the firehouse across the street, where Jimmy, the fire fighter, had shown them around. All the children had sat in the truck, tried on boots and hats, and examined the sliding pole. Malik and Nicole were frightened of the siren and so those two left before Caitlin tried it out. It had seemed to Jimmy and the other fire fighters like any other preschool outing to the firehouse. But as the group was preparing to leave, Caitlin said, "So, Jimmy, when are you going to get a woman fire fighter around here?" Caitlin and her friends Megan and Britt, as well as several other children, had been interested all year in the news that women were becoming fire fighters in New York. JoAnne had brought in pictures from newspapers and magazines of the women in training, graduating from the fire academy, joining their engine companies, fighting their first fires. The children had made little books by cutting out the pictures, pasting them onto construction paper, and dictating captions for each one. Furthermore, everyone Caitlin knew used the nonsexist term "fire fighter" in preference to "fireman." One of the little wooden figures called wedgies in the block area was a woman fire fighter, and one of the mommies in the *Mommies Can Do Anything* book was a fire fighter.

And yet, changing language does not in itself change reality. As a child, as a concrete learner, as a person who bases her knowledge on experience, it was clear and undeniable to Caitlin and the others that across the street there were only firemen. And the little wedgies notwithstanding, the firemen were all white. Caitlin's sense of fairness was with the struggle of the courageous women fire fighters, and since everyone she knew agreed on that, it seemed obvious to her that everyone agreed. And so Caitlin, innocently holding Jimmy's hand, looked up at her friend and said, "So, Jimmy, when are you going to get a woman fire fighter around here?" Jimmy's response was not encouraging.

"Women?" he roared. "I hope never. We don't want any women here." The kids were shocked; Jimmy tried to explain.

"Listen, this is dangerous work and it's hard. This is not work for a woman."

Caitlin and Megan were holding hands now. "This isn't fair," said Caitlin angrily. "Yeah," Megan said. "Women can do anything." Encouraged, Caitlin added, "I hope women fire fighters come here and they don't let any men in."

Jimmy, staggered slightly by the force and heat of this sudden argument, retreated into his laugh. "Never happen," he said hopefully. "If women take over, the neighborhood will burn down."

Back at school they wrote lots of letters to the women fire fighters, the station house, the fire commissioner, and the mayor.

Caitlin finds the picture of herself, glasses, smile, and braids obscured beneath the heavy, oversized fire hat. "Here I am," she announces, and places it in the pile with Zaida Gonzales. The trip to the firehouse happened long ago, but Caitlin remembers it vividly—the argument, the letters she wrote afterward, the encouragement from her family and friends as she was asked to tell and retell the now famous tale.

By now Jared, Britt, and Misha have arrived and joined in sorting and commenting on the pictures from the folders. "Here's my mom picking strawberries," says Britt, holding up a snapshot of her mother on a hillside of green. "And here's JJ singing." The picture is of a rock band in full eruption, guitars blazing, drums pounding, and a female singer, JJ—who also worked for awhile part-time at the day-care center—twisting, leaping, blasting into a microphone.

"I started doing these bulletin boards a few years ago around different themes," JoAnne explains. "In March, I do a collage for International Women's Day. It began as a multi-cultural display of women in nontraditional roles and of some famous women fighters, like this poster of Harriet Tubman. The parents like it, but more interesting to me was that the kids really responded to it. They'd come out here in the hall, pull a chair over, and point out their favorites. So the next year I incorporated pictures of their mothers and baby-sitters and women friends into the collage, and it grew into what it is now."

JoAnne begins stapling up the pictures, paintings, and photographs, and as she does patterns emerge and suggest themselves to her. Caitlin and Britt stay with the project, mulling over pictures, handing around candidates, straightening up. Other kids go in and out for short periods. "Jared," JoAnne says, "Why don't you go paint a picture for Women's Day and I'll tape it over here next to the bulletin board." Jared runs into the room and returns moments later with a piece of large newsprint dripping with paint, a blue circle with two dots for eyes, a line mouth, and two straight-line legs coming right out of the head—a typical three-year-old's tadpole person. "Write, 'To All Women,'" says Jared. JoAnne writes the words, saying them aloud as she does, and tapes the painting up on the wall. Several other kids decide to paint tributes to Women's Day. Micco paints a circle, two dots, a mouth, and two straight-line arms as well as two legs. And Sanaya, whose mother is Indian, paints a head with eyes, hair, and a smudge of red on the forehead; a body; a triangular skirt, and legs. Her painting says, "It's a Tika on her forehead. She's from India. That woman is me."

The bulletin board collage has grown into a festive celebration of women. There is a large painting of Sojourner Truth with her famous exhortation about the role of women:

> The man over there says that women need to be helped into carriages and lifted over ditches. . . . Nobody ever helps me into carriages or over puddles . . . and ain't I a woman? Look at my arm! I have ploughed and planted and gathered into barns, and no man could head me . . . and ain't I a woman? I have borne thirteen children, and seen most of them sold into slavery, and when I cried out with my mother's grief, none but Jesus heard me . . . and ain't I a woman?

And there is a larger-than-life portrait of a black woman's head surrounded by red roses against a blazing orange background with the words "Bread and Roses" emblazoned across it.

There is a picture of one mother operating a television camera next to another nursing her baby. There is an ancient-looking picture of one child's mother setting off to climb Mount Kilimanjaro. One mother is shooting a free throw in a basketball game, another is drinking a victory beer at the finish of a footrace, and a third is demonstrating a karate punch. Malik's mother is giving a speech, Tracy's mother is being interviewed on TV, Jean's mother is acting on the stage, Dylan's mother is receiving an award. There is a grandmother on the Hopi reservation, another in India, one in Jamaica, one in Cuba, one in Israel, and one in Guatemala.

And there are lots of pictures of mothers mothering. "Here I am when I was a baby with Mommy and Cutie Dog," says Misha. "And here I am with Mommy, my grandma, and my great-grandma." Four generations of women.

There are young women and old women, women working and women at play, known women and unknown women, women in familiar places and women in unfamiliar settings, women from here and women from almost anywhere. As the collage grows, a rich and varied, broad and powerful portrait of women emerges. Energy and possibilities. But its effect is not overpowering to Max. "Here's my mom with my baby brother at the hospital," he says, pointing to a snapshot in the middle of the swirling, joyful color.

Caitlin and Britt and JoAnne straighten up, putting away staplers, tape, and extra pictures. The are done for now, but the board is not finished. As families bring in more pictures, they will be absorbed into the collage and become part of the collection. It will grow and change, a living thing for a month or so, and then will be stored in fat folders for next year.

"I'm often asked, 'Aren't these kids much too young to be aware of social issues?'" JoAnne says later. "'Aren't you frightening them with things they can't really understand?' I don't think so; in fact, my whole experience with young children tells me the opposite." She pauses for a moment.

"I think that children's natural fascination with the world knows no limits. They don't go exploring and then stop when they come to a social question. Rather, they're intensely interested in groups, in their families, friends, strangers, other kids. And at a very young age kids begin to socialize, to be interested in themselves in relation to others, in group play. Of course, they're still self-centered, but they develop rapidly into an awareness of their own limits as well as their own rights. Three-year-olds have a pretty strong sense of what's fair and what's unfair, and that sense isn't always self-serving.

"I'm not advocating lecturing to kids," she adds. "I think kids learn mainly through everyday, concrete experiences. But I don't think we can be timid about these things either. All the research shows that very young kids, two or three years old, already know that there are sexual and racial differences, whether they're talked about or not. They know from their experience in the world. By four or five, kids know that in our society one is superior and the other inferior. Because they know these things already, what is the effect of not mentioning it? In their eyes, it's not neutral; it's evasive and it's accepting.

"I'm interested in empowering kids in all aspects of their lives," JoAnne continues, "And kids can't be powerful if we pretend that the things they see and feel aren't real. I mean, go and ask a random group of four-year-olds about war and nuclear weapons and you'll hear the most frightening, overpowering images. And yet, how many four-year-olds can also say 'I talked to my Mom and she says good people can stop the war; we wrote a letter against war and went on a march.'"

JoAnne tells a story of taking a walk with four children and passing the window of a toy store where a large, stuffed panda bear wearing an Indian headdress sat on a wooden rocking horse. "Look, JoAnne," Megan said. "That makes fun of Native Americans." Megan had been told that "playing Indians" was not the same as playing doctor or pilot or circus, because an Indian was not a job or a role, but a member of a group of human beings. To "play Indian" was to trivialize and caricature a people and a culture; it was unfair and it hurt their feelings.

They went into the store and Megan told the manager, "You should take that off." After some discussions the manager got a ladder and took the headdress off. As they were leaving, Megan, delighted and victorious, said, "We helped change that store."

"I want kids to feel that they can speak right up, say something to change things for the better," JoAnne says. "I want them to feel that people can be effective and powerful. Kids have an emerging strong sense of justice and I don't want it crushed. I remember walking with some kids and seeing a drunk sleeping in the gutter. 'What's wrong?' they asked. 'Why is he lying in the street? What are we going to do?' It took us quite awhile to find a cop and tell him about the man in the street. If I'd been alone I'd have walked away, but the kids could not accept that we would just leave him there. And I think they were right."

JoAnne asked several kids to complete the sentence, "A woman is . . ." Mwaniki smiled and said, "A woman is Nancy. A woman likes to go to work. Women like to paint. They like to pick tomatoes." Malik answered, "A woman is Mommy. A woman is my friend." And Britt said earnestly, "A woman is a mother, a teacher, a producer, a police, an engineer, a motor girl, a zookeeper, a housekeeper, a baby-sitter. A work woman can be anything she wants to be. She can choose. Women like to work and relax."

JoAnne transcribed these dictations, copied them onto heavy sheets of paper, and is now hanging them near the women's collage.

"I do a lot of interviewing," JoAnne says. "The kids like that word 'interview.' So when I say, 'I want to interview you,' I always draw a crowd. But to be effective I have to do it one at a time. In a group they imitate each other too much, and repeat what they hear one another say, and I can't get a sense of what each one is thinking."

There are other sets of interviews filed away. One is a mimeographed questionnaire: "My name is ———. I am ——— years old. I live ———. I live with ———. One of my favorite colors is ———. One of my favorite foods is ———. One thing that makes me happy is ———. One thing that makes me sad is ———. One of my favorite songs is ———." This simple form not only elicited differences in preferences (food: rice and beans; pork chops; french fries and ketchup; sweet gherkins; Chinese food; candy) and living styles (I live with: my family; Mom and Dad; Susan and Steve and Renee) but also in levels of understanding (I live: at 520 West 123rd Street; in New York; in a room; I forgot; or, A friend is: someone you play with; you; JoAnne; Mommy). The questionnaire provided insights into the feelings and thoughts of several of the children. Asked to think of one thing that makes him happy, one child said with a smile, "Mommy"; asked to think of one thing that makes him sad, the same child frowned and said "Mommy" again.

"I'm not focused on this because they say cute things," JoAnne says, "even though a lot of what they say is unique, sometimes funny, and sometimes brilliant. But the importance of it is that kids are thinking deeply about their world, and when you work with young kids you want to find ways for them to express their thoughts and feelings through play and any other means you can set up. These interviews are useful to me. I try to listen and watch carefully so I understand each one better."

JoAnne pulls other dictations from a folder. One says, "When I dream at night I dream about ————." Misha said, "Nightmares. They're scary. They have big teeth and big feet. They're real quiet. I tell them to go away. They don't wear clothes. If they go to Cutie Dog's bed, I go to her bed and tell her the nightmares are not scary." Sanaya answered, "I dream about Christmas and the Christmas tree." Chesa said, "I dream about animals. I dream about tigers and bears and all kinds of animals. They're scary dreams. Deer come into my bed and they sleep with me."

Earlier, JoAnne transcribed some questions for Santa Claus: "Why is your tummy so ho, ho, ho? Can I live in your house? Is your skin from Africa? Why are you old? What do you play with? Do you know my baby brother can crawl?"

JoAnne's written records are dictations, children's paintings and drawings, and the information sheets periodically written to parents describing an activity or event. But what she relies on are her individual relationships with each child. "I should take more notes," she admits. "But time and energy are a factor. Still, I'm confident that I know in detail where every kid is developmentally because I make it my business to know each one intimately."

When asked to describe the reward of teaching for her, JoAnne responds immediately: Hutch, Ellen, Isadora, Timineet, Megan, Caitlin, Britt, Henry—the names of children she has known, cared for, and taught. And with each name there is an enthusiastic story or incident or detail. Megan, for example:

"I love it when kids are passionate about anything, and Megan is a kid who was passionate about many things. She had a wide range of interests, she loved dramatic play and art, she loved to be read to, and she became a great reader. She was always concerned about fairness, and we talked about what seemed fair and unfair to her a lot. We had an especially close relationship, and her parents asked me to be responsible for her during the birth of her brother at the Maternity Center. Megan and I read and talked and played and took walks, and we were there when Max was born. Megan said, 'Look how strong my mom is—look at her muscles.' I thought, 'What a powerful experience for a daughter to have of her mother.' I was glad that Megan could have such a positive experience, that she could be so relaxed at such a stressful time; and I felt that I made a difference there."

JoAnne has made a difference in hundreds of families, developing special expertise in preparing children for the birth of a sibling, helping kids cope with a hospitalization, dealing with problems like a death in the family, divorce, separation, and physical disabilities. She has had experience in working with kids who were troubled about their interracial identities, and in supporting children who had a parent in prison. These are some of JoAnne's "specialities."

At Hunter Elementary School, where she is now a student, Megan was given the Susan B. Anthony award recently for helping to promote equality between boys and girls. She told her mother that JoAnne deserved part of it, and they made a copy to give to her. JoAnne says, "That was a shining moment for me." She continues, "Megan is what I'd like a daughter to be: engaged, bright, strong inside herself, wide-awake, and committed. She enriches everything around her. She feels all the options are open to her and that she can accomplish anything. For a girl, that's a great thing. I feel somewhat responsible for that, and what's more, she feels that I'm somewhat responsible. That delights me."

JoAnne's map of her pathway to teaching reaches back to Palmyra, New York, the small upstate community where she was raised, and Rochester, the big city where she lived and worked after high school. When she decided to move to New York City at the age of 26 it represented to her a break from the constraints and limitations of her life, a step into something unknown and challenging, a move that was daring and a little offbeat. Her model was "That Girl," the TV comedy starring Marlo Thomas about the experiences of a working woman in New York City. Marlo Thomas was cool and independent, and JoAnne would be cool and independent. People in Palmyra, she thought, would be shocked and yet grudgingly respectful of what she would become.

JoAnne came to New York as a volunteer in a political campaign, and she worked as a receptionist. She lived in a hotel for women and remembers going to Greenwich Village almost immediately to get a haircut and new clothes. The women's hotel addressed one of the regrets she had about not going to college: It was a community of women, full of fun and all-night talks. After the campaign ended she worked as a secretary and later as an assistant to an oral surgeon. "I thrive on responsibility," she says now, "and I couldn't stay on this last job because I had no sense that what I did mattered. Anyway, I was about to turn 30 and I thought, 'Well, I'm going to be a grown-up soon, what do I want to do?' I left that job and looked for what was next."

JoAnne soon met a young family in the laundry room of her building. The mother, Jane, asked her if she would baby-sit, and JoAnne, who had never baby-sat in high school and never thought of kids as part of her life, agreed. This became a turning-point experience. "Hutch was a year old and my first day with him I was hooked. Jane trusted me with her child and that struck me, and Hutch was just a joy to be with. I began baby-sitting more and more. I'd meet people in the building or the park, and eventually every day was filled with different baby-sitting jobs. For the first time in my life I liked getting up at seven and I looked forward to work. I had a growing sense that I had found my spot."

Jane became JoAnne's teacher, and JoAnne remembers Jane's saying and doing things that would later become important in her own work. "Jane was a relaxed mother, enthusiastic and confident, and that helped to relax me. Jane didn't think of motherhood as a dreary accident, or time with Hutch as dull and stupid. She always told me I was a natural with kids and to trust myself. At the same time she was bringing me books and articles about child development to read, she would say, 'You don't need this, but you'll see how much you already know.' She was affirming and empowering, qualities that are central in my own teaching."

Jane was a nurse as well as a mother, and JoAnne felt particularly happy that Jane had so much confidence in her. Jane argued that JoAnne should take on child care as more than a baby-sitting job and should see it as a worthy professional commitment. With Jane's help JoAnne began to see taking care of children as valuable, loving labor, something that was both complex and urgently needed.

JoAnne describes this as a period of excitement, growth, and change for her: "I began to baby-sit for lots of people. My phone rang off the hook, and soon I was taking care of kids every day, every night, and weekends. In my spare time I talked to Jane, and she kept saying that this was my calling, what I was meant to do. I found the whole experience exhilarating. I remember one time early on, it just happened that I had Hutch and Eric on the same day because their mothers asked me, and I was fascinated by the interaction between them. It wasn't some kind of underdeveloped, superficial play that you might read about. I was amazed at how full and engaged it was. I'd never realized before that there could be relationships among kids this young. So now I was on the way to group care. I bought a little red wagon that could hold three kids for walks or trips to the park."

JoAnne continued to go on job interviews, but her heart wasn't in it. She felt fully alive and needed with the children, and the interviews became a formality, necessary for the unemployment. She saw, too, that the need for child care was intense and that she could perhaps make a living doing it.

"The decisive moment," she recalls, "came when I was offered a job in a fancy downtown office as secretary to the manager of the rock group KISS. A few months before, this would have been the fulfillment of a dream: the rock world, lots of glitz, famous people, and $250 a week. I could hardly believe I was turning it down. It didn't even sound like my voice. My friend John McGowan, who got me the interview, will never get over it. Jane was so happy she cried. She said I was right, and I thought I was right. She said I'd make a real contribution and that this would be an important project. I hoped so."

Later, JoAnne put this "decisive moment" in perspective: "For 10 years now my teaching has been my life. There has been very little separation between the two. When I began in my apartment, I was living and working in the same space. I would often be working into the night, fixing things up for the next day, changing the wall hangings, and preparing. It was hard for me to leave. There always seemed to be something I could do. Even when we moved locations, it was difficult for me to leave when my work hours were over. My entire group of friends that I see outside of school are people that I met through the school in some way. I have always socialized with the parents and some of the staff."

She continues, "When I began this work, my friends seemed to wonder why I was doing this, how I could stand to take care of little kids all day, what about the money? I found we had little in common any more, once they began thinking of climbing the corporate ladder and I was excited about seeing Hutch learn how to walk. So we drifted apart."

Every morning at eight the strollers would arrive and line up in the hallway outside her apartment. Although she took only five children at a time, she had twenty-five children attending a complicated schedule represented on a graph hanging above her bed. She worked from eight in the morning until six in the evening and still baby-sat evenings and weekends. "I had a lot of energy because it was all new and exciting," she explains. "And I felt I had to baby-sit so that people would know me and trust me." After nine months of this, she knew she would have to move out of her apartment and that somehow the program would have to change.

She told everyone she knew that she was looking for space, and within a few days one of the mothers in the program called to say she'd seen an empty brownstone two blocks from JoAnne's apartment. The building belonged to the Farmworkers' Union, and JoAnne spoke to the two nuns who were in residence there and wrote to Caesar Chavez about using the ground floor as a day-care center. Weeks went by without response, and JoAnne organized all the families to write and send telegrams describing the need for day care and what a "good cause" it was. Finally Chavez agreed, and JoAnne moved her day-care center into the first home of its own. "It never would have survived without the Farmworkers coming through when they did," JoAnne says. "It was a miracle." While she attributes several turning points on her pathway to teaching to chance, it is often, as in this case, chance sprinkled with a lot of intention, hard work, and organizing ability. "I've always lived not knowing what was next, and yet I tend to think that things will work out." Her iron will plays more of a part in that optimistic conclusion than she ever acknowledges.

At about this time JoAnne met a woman outside her building who asked if she needed help caring for all her children. When JoAnne explained that none of the children were hers, the woman laughed and explained that her own eighteen-year-old daughter, who was coming to New York and was good with children, needed a job. JoAnne met Corrine and hired her almost instantly. "Corrine was intuitively great with kids," JoAnne says. "She was lively and self-starting. She changed my life because suddenly it was much easier, safer, and more fun. I was less isolated, and I had someone to compare notes with. I thought, 'What would I have done if anything had gone wrong when I was alone?' I often think if I'd known all that was involved—the dangers as well as the licensing and money hassles—I'd never have begun. But youthful ignorance and luck allowed it to happen. Corrine was another miracle and another indication that this was meant to happen."

When asked if she was surprised to find herself teaching, she responds, "If anyone had ever told me that this is what I'd become, I'd never have believed it. But it felt right from the first moment, and that gave me the courage to keep going. And once I'd made the decision, all the ambivalence and ambiguity went away, and there was no stopping me."

JoAnne remembers playing school with neighborhood children when she was a child. She always had a pointer and a chalkboard. "One of the few child-centered things my mother did was to make sure we always had sand in the sandbox, swings, chalk, and a chalkboard. I don't have a very integrated memory of my mother, because while there are bright spots, there are also long periods of her neglect and anger. In one way she was a strong person and a doer, someone whom no one walked on. Ironically, I trace some of my feminist feelings to her. When a neighbor's house burned down, my mother organized the community effort to help the family. But now I think of her when I was six—with me, a three-year-old, an eighteen-month-old, a newborn baby, and a husband who drank, and still running her beauty shop in the enclosed front porch—and I can see where some of that anger came from. But as a child I was often frightened and confused, and she was often withdrawn. My mother acted like I couldn't get my life together, and she never trusted me, although I don't remember giving her any reason for not trusting me. Sometimes now if I say something disapproving to a child, I hear my mother's voice and that scares me. As a child I turned to my teachers, who liked me and let me be a safety patrol, a messenger, or a monitor. I remember several of my early teachers vividly because I adopted each of them, and they replaced my mother in my affection."

Later JoAnne thought more about the impact of her life on her work and sent me the following note:

"When I first began to work with young children, I did a lot of reading on child development. I had no idea that what happened to you when you were young affected your adulthood. I must have known it, but I didn't understand how greatly it could affect your whole life. The more I read, the more I thought about my own childhood. I pulled up memories I hadn't thought of in years. I began to talk to my two sisters, and they told me things I had totally blocked out. I began to wonder how I survived childhood and adolescence at all. I must have gotten a great deal of love, nurturing, and cuddling in the first three years because my parents had tried to have a baby for ten years. My mother had told me the story of how wanted I was and how thrilled she was when she became pregnant. So I am assuming I was nurtured in the beginning.

"But my overwhelming memory of my mother is her telling me I was irresponsible, not smart enough, wrong. I had such a feeling of being bad that it is still with me today. I have given a lot of thought to what patterns begin at a young age and remain with you. So if you look at the 'Goals for Children' I recently wrote, you will see they are really goals for everyone. They are not something you work on in high school to prepare for the real world; they are goals you begin to develop in infancy. They are always on my mind when I am at school or thinking about the day or preparing for the next day, in conferences, while planning activities, or when talking about kids with the staff. I refer to them constantly.

"When I say something to a child that reminds me of my mother, I cringe and think, 'How can I rephrase that to foster a positive feeling?' I want to let the child know it is what she is *doing* that is unacceptable or hurtful to someone else, not that she *is* bad.

"When I look back at the way I grew up thinking I couldn't draw, because someone told me I couldn't, or at how I wasn't encouraged to be good in math or science, or at how I wasn't smart enough to take out a loan to be sent to college like my sister, or at how I was never encouraged to ice skate even though my father was a professional hockey player in Canada and spent weekends teaching my school friends (boys) how to play hockey, I get so angry at the options that were never open for me. I want more than anything to open all the doors to the kids I care for. I think that is the important impact I can have on their lives, because so many of those doors are shut down before the kids enter kindergarten."

JoAnne remembers important details from her relationships with several teachers: Miss Tucker's father making a brightly colored wooden shoe on which the children practiced tying laces, and how proud she felt and how much she loved Miss Tucker for showing her how; Miss Wheeler coming to the hospital after JoAnne had had her tonsils out and bringing her homework, which made her feel important and overjoyed; Mrs. Alvarez coming to her mother's shop to get her hair done and then coming one night with her son for dinner. Starting in kindergarten, JoAnne dreaded the end of each year and the inevitable separation from her adopted mother-substitute. In these memories there are themes that resonate in JoAnne's teaching: a sense of embracing a child as a whole person, an attempt to communicate a feeling of specialness to each child, a desire to empower children to be competent and whole members of their communities, and an effort to acknowledge and grow from the necessity of separation.

"It builds confidence in kids if adults trust them," JoAnne says. "That's why I look for ways to give them real work to do, like getting the mail or taking messages to the other room." One day the phone rang in the day-care center, and Henry, four years old, answered, spoke for a few minutes, and then hung up. JoAnne asked who it was, and Henry replied, "It was Gigi, and she wanted to know if Cameron was up from his nap yet. I said he'd had a good nap, and she said she'd come by after she went running." JoAnne beamed as Henry told her about the conversation.

Cameron is two years old, and he's been in the day-care center for only a couple of months. When he first arrived, the other children were helpful and welcoming. "I love it when I see the kids expressing empathy for others," JoAnne says. "I feel like we've created an environment that encourages a natural kind of caring and compassion, and that makes me happy." On his third day of day care, Cameron's mother felt he was comfortable enough for her to leave. After Cameron waved good-bye from the window, a ritual that JoAnne thinks helps separations since the parent is already physically separated but can still be seen, Henry took Cameron's hand, without any adult encouragement, and led him to the block area to build. As they worked, Henry said, "They always come back." Max added, "Sometimes I get lonely but I know it's okay." Cameron watched and listened. When he woke up from his nap, Henry touched him gently and said, "Today was your first nap," and Max added, "And you're still here." It was a cuddly, nurturing moment, a lovely moment in which the sense of caring was evident and pervasive.

Empowerment for JoAnne is more than a handy slogan. She recently spent many extra hours raising money to convert the bathroom into one with a child-sized toilet and sink. "They need a bathroom they can function in," she says. "Every time the kids asked me for help turning on the water it was a slap in the face for them." JoAnne spends considerable time each year teaching young children how to pour their own juice and put on their own coats "the magic way," because she believes that these are the empowering issues for two-, three-, and four-year-olds. In her classroom there is a snack table with crackers and cheese, carrots, and juice always available and within reach. "What could be more basic than to regulate your own feeding?" JoAnne asks rhetorically. "And yet how many adults let kids decide if and when they're hungry? Here they can eat when they're hungry and stop eating when they're full. That's a basic issue of independence and trust, like having tissues within their reach and accessible toilets. Having a set snack time that all youngsters are supposed to conform to disempowers kids, just like having a toileting time does."

On a deeper level JoAnne believes that this kind of empowerment leads to children being able to take responsibility for ever-widening areas of their lives. Trusting children to know when they're hungry is a step toward trusting them to know when they're sad, when they're angry, and when they're ecstatic, and to take responsibility for those feelings as well. JoAnne has been in therapy for two years and thinks that that process has made her a better teacher, more confident, more certain of her own worth, more aware of her own feelings, and therefore more able to help children be in touch with themselves.

One of JoAnne's special loves is reading, and she takes tremendous pride in her extensive collections of quality books for children. "Books are my passion. I look for a good story when I'm buying a book," says JoAnne. "I don't really care if the publisher thinks it's only for six-year-olds. If a book is too wordy, I'll leave parts out or change words to make the story available. Often, even if kids don't get every word, they follow along and get the general idea. I can tell if something is working for them because they ask for it again and again. Two popular books this year have been *The Drinking Gourd*, a story about the Underground Railroad and how some white people fought slavery too, and *Running with Rachel*, a story about a girl's experience with jogging and racing. Both books were listed for older children, and yet both were read and reread here."

The closet holds hundreds of children's books on labeled shelves. The "General Story" shelf includes *The Very Hungry Caterpillar*, *Where the Wild Things Are*, and *Make Way for Ducklings*. But there are no books by Richard Scarry, one of the most popular, best-selling children's authors. "I don't like his books," says JoAnne flatly. "They're full of stereotypes of women, and almost every book ridicules Native American dress or culture. *Busy, Busy World* manages to have a stupid Mexican character, a sly Arab, and a Chinese character named Ah-Choo. Scarry's books are just offensive."

The book collection has depth and variety: There is a book about a day in the life of a modern Navajo girl who lives on a reservation, another about weaving a rug from wool, and another about a boy becoming a dancer. There are books on disabilities, separations and divorce, the loss of a loved one, adoption, parents in prison, childhood fears, interracial identity, and more. There is a large shelf of books labeled "Anti-Racist" and another "Anti-Sexist." "Kids are bombarded by white, male images all day long," JoAnne says. "This is an alternative. It helps balance it out. And I don't think of it only as giving female, black, and Third World kids a positive self-image. To me it's important that boys see girls—women—in a variety of strong roles, and that the white kids see black people in a positive way."

JoAnne pulls a book from the shelf. "Every classroom needs this book," she says, holding up *Honey, I Love*, by Eloise Greenfield. It is a book of poems about love and the experiences of children. Each page is illustrated with a beautiful charcoal portrait of a black girl, and a panorama in the style of a child's painting. JoAnne puts on a record of *Honey, I Love*, which Eloise Greenfield made with a chorus of seven children and some jazz musicians led by Byron Morris. The poems are transformed into street chants, jump rope rhymes, blues numbers, ragtime, swing, improvisation. "Riding on the Train" becomes a child's view of the countryside with brushes drumming lightly to the rhythm; "Rope Rhyme" becomes a rhumba with chorus. "The content, the sound, the images, the illustrations, the variety of positive black hairstyles—it all adds up to a remarkable book," says JoAnne.

JoAnne believes that there is a book that can address practically any problem and a book that can speak to any child, and she thinks she should be able to make the match or write one of her own if none exists. When asked recently to shape a symbol of her teaching out of clay, JoAnne created a figure of herself with two small people on her lap and an open book spread out before them.

Books are one part of an element that JoAnne considers central to her teaching: the need for dialogue. "I try to respond to every child. I reach out, and the kids I have difficulty with are the ones who don't respond, who can't connect. That's one advantage of team teaching, because if I can't connect with someone, chances are that Denise or Andrea can."

JoAnne claims that she can remember the exact moment when the first important connection was made with each child. Sarah, for example, "asked me to undo her overalls so she could go to the bathroom. A little later she came to me and asked me to help her do up her pants the right way because, while someone buttoned them, the person had failed to twist the straps so they wouldn't keep slipping down. She didn't have the words to describe the problem, but I could see what was wrong, and as I worked on it, I told her that I remembered from when I was a little girl that the straps needed to be twisted. She looked at me intently and said 'Tell me more about when you were a little girl.' We talked off and on all day about when I was a little girl, and by the end of the day we were deep friends. She told her parents some of the stories that night, and that was the beginning with Sarah."

When JoAnne thought more about dialogue, she wrote:

"I have always cringed when I visited another center and heard teachers speaking to kids in a 'teacher voice.' It is patronizing and disrespectful. I don't even like to hear baby talk spoken to infants. I always try to speak to children in an honest, respectful manner.

"Often, adults think children who don't talk don't understand, but I think children understand long before they talk. I don't think we should talk about children to others in their presence, without acknowledging them—we shouldn't discuss them with others as if they weren't there. They hear, they understand, they feel.

"I try to listen when a child is talking, really listen, and I try to look the child in the eye. I help children in a group; each has a chance to talk. Jake has a hard time getting his words out when he is excited, and other children often lose patience waiting, so we remind them it is Jake's turn and they can talk later. I try to remember to say 'please' and 'thank you' to them, when appropriate, instead of insisting they use those phrases. I think they will learn to be polite to others by having others be polite to them.

"I think the children I know have large vocabularies because they are read to a great deal, they are talked to and listened to with respect, and we encourage them to talk, question, and offer their opinions and ideas.

"When I was nine my mom took me to the police station because someone said I threw a rock at a window. I hadn't done it and I was scared and humiliated, but she wouldn't believe me. It was always that way with her: Someone else was right, teachers were right, books were right. I want kids to know themselves well enough to speak up with ease and confidence. I want them to have a passion for books, but I also want them to be critical readers."

When JoAnne reads to children she always starts with the title and then the author's name and the illustrator's name, and sometimes she reads a few words from the biographical sketches in the back, as if to underline the fact that this book was written by someone and that that someone had a point of view. When children dictate their own stories, JoAnne includes a section called "About the Author."

JoAnne thinks that what is valuable in her teaching is that she respects children, talks to them as if they were fully human, and assumes an intelligence in children. "This may sound obvious, but I'm still amazed at how often kids are bullied, patronized, and ignored in our society," she says. Her goals for children include each one developing a sense of fairness and self-respect, confidence and inner happiness.

The space in the center is laid out to reflect these same goals, for it is open and flexible, with maximum possibilities for child construction and de-construction. A large, narrow room opens into a tremendous dress-up area, where children give concrete expression to their observations and experiences of the world. There is a large block area and a low table without chairs so kids can work on the smooth, flat surface or use it as a barrier to crawl under and clamber over. There is water and sand, a cozy library, tables for eating, and fish tanks and animals. It's a comfortable, relaxed, home-like room with only the barest outline of a routine, which evolves and changes slowly. There is a drop-off time and a pick-up time, a community gathering before lunch, and nap time after lunch, but there are also months when small groups go to the playground almost every morning, and other months when the American Museum of Natural History becomes a favorite haunt to explore day after day.

Britt, Misha, and Sanaya are crowded around the tape recorder listening to Sanaya's grandmother sing a lullaby: "Nini baba nini/ Makhan roti chini/ Makhan roti kha gaza/ Baba so gaza." As she sings, they sing along, Sanaya smiling dreamily. "When my grandma sang this I was this big," says Sanaya, scrunching up her face and holding her hands just inches apart. "Smaller than an ant." And later, "It's in Hindi. I can sing Hindi."

"I sang this all weekend," says Britt, "and I thought about you, Sanaya."

JoAnne is making a birthday card for Malik, gathering greetings and salutations from his friends: "You're my friend, Malik. You never hurt me." "Happy Birthday, Malik." "I like you Malik." Jorge has painted a smiling red face for Malik and dictated "Feliz Cumpleaños, Malik."

Denise is reading Eloise Greenfield's *African Dream* to a group in the book corner. Mwaniki says, "My dad's from Africa. This is about me." The book ends with a grandmother rocking a child to sleep. Sanaya shouts, "That's just like me and 'Nini baba nini.'"

"We are child-centered here," JoAnne says. "We are conscious of the development of the whole child, emotions and feelings, minds and bodies. But no child comes isolated from society and culture. To be truly child-centered is also to be conscious of culture and involved in society."

JoAnne is involved in a multitude of projects outside her own day-care center, but in her own mind they are all linked together. "One of my greatest concerns is war and the threat of war. I want a healthy and peaceful world, and I work for that here in the center. One of the great contradictions for me is the pervasiveness of violent play and war toys. I know that kids need to feel powerful, and in a world that renders kids and all of us powerless and at risk, superheroes and war toys become particularly seductive. When a kid solves a problem, I'll try to remember to say something like, 'Max, you really solved that problem!' I feel that I can't in good faith stifle Max's turning everything into a gun and rushing about the room shooting everything, but I can't allow that energy to take over either. One thing I try to do is to humanize the bad guys. I might say, 'Let's write a book about Darth Vader's mom,' or 'Let's pretend Skeletor is going to the dentist today,' or 'Do Phantom's kids think he's a bad guy?' This changes the play. Or I might say, 'Let's read the book about Harriet Tubman, who was a real superhero.'"

High on the walls are life-sized brown paper cutouts of each child which have been individually decorated and hung up. Each has a different shape and texture. Malik's is painted red and blue and has tinsel and ribbon glued on it. Mee Hyun's has just a dash of paint. Sanaya's is covered with painted circles, each with a button or piece of material glued neatly into the center. Jorge's feels like the child himself, running, leaping off the wall. And Britt's is bold and colorful, with paint and styrofoam and lace defining eyes, mouth, hair, toes; her name is painted backwards along one arm. There are several posters decorating the walls: a black grandmother sitting on the steps of a porch scattered with brightly colored plastic toys, hugging a laughing child on her lap; the famous photograph of Rosa Parks being booked for refusing to stand up on the bus; a picture of Martin Luther King, Jr. and Malcolm X in an enthusiastic embrace.

One morning as JoAnne is setting up the room, she says, "You know, I'm tired of looking at the pictures on the wall."

"What do you mean?" asks Britt.

"Well, those horses have been over the easel for months. I need a change of scenery. Let's change the room around."

"Okay," says Britt eagerly.

"You don't want to take our silhouettes down, do you?" asks Sanaya. "No," says JoAnne. "I'd just like to see some new posters or paintings. Do you want to put up some of your paintings?" "No! No! No!"

"Well, then, let's see what's in the closet. You can help me make the decisions."

There's that word again. Suddenly the whole room is crackling with energy and crowding into the closet to make decisions. JoAnne pulls out five fat rolls of posters and puts them on the floor. She takes one roll to the table and opens it. Several kids pick through the posters, admiring, judging, commenting. "Oh, that's beautiful." "I like this one because of the color." "I don't like that one."

There are several pictures of Martin Luther King, Jr. in the first roll. "Should we take Martin Luther King down?" Britt asks. "I don't know," says JoAnne. "Do you want to leave him up a while longer?" "Is his birthday over?" asks Britt. "Yes." "Well them, let's take him down," says Sanaya. "Okay."

"Now let's make another decision," says Jared happily.

They find a giant folded poster in the closet and open it up carefully. It is a collage of 31 black-and-white photographs of different families, and under each one is written: "We are a family." Britt's eyes widen and she shouts excitedly, "There's one like my family." JoAnne brings the poster out of the closet and spreads it out over the table for everyone to examine. There is an amazing diversity of families here: a woman in the laundromat with her son, six people watching TV, a man in a wheelchair with his wife and three daughters, a woman kneading bread in front of a family portrait, a Native American man surrounded by his children.

Mwaniki comes up, looks for a few seconds, and says, "Look, they're just like me. See, the father's black and the mother's white."

"Where?" asks Jared. "Oh, there I am."

"But I'm blacker than that kid," says Mwaniki. "I'm more Africa."

Misha comes and finds a family with a small dog. "That's my family," she says.

Everyone wants this one up for sure. "Where will we put it?" asks JoAnne. "It's so big; it's bigger than any of our bulletin boards." They look around the room. Someone suggests the chalkboard. "Okay," says Jo-Anne. "But that will mean not using the chalkboard for awhile. And we'll have to remind everyone so that people don't draw on this poster."

The poster is taped to the chalkboard. Then JoAnne digs out from the closet a series of 8-1/2 × 11 cardboard-backed photographs of different families, and Sanaya, Britt, and Mwaniki begin sorting through them. "We should put this one up," says Sanaya, holding up an Asian family, "for Mee Hyun." "And let's put this grandma up," says Britt. Soon another wall is decorated with photographs of different families.

"Now I want to draw my family," says Britt. She goes to the table with a big sheet of paper, takes a crayon, and draws a circle in the center of the page with eyes, two pointed ears, and four legs. "That's my cat," she says. She draws two big tadpole people and two little ones with triangular skirts. "A family is who you live with. A family loves you. A family takes care of you. My family is going for a walk."

Jorge draws three flying figures with long arms and legs trailing behind. Max uses a separate page for each family member, carefully etching in hair, eyebrows, hands, and feet in different proportions and arrangements.

"Let's tell your parents to bring in some pictures of you and your families, and we'll decorate this wall with all of our families," says JoAnne. She makes a sign and tapes it up above some blank space: "These Are Our Families."

Jorge says, "I have a big book of pictures at home from when I was a baby to now. I'll bring them in. And I'll bring my cat's picture."

"Let's make another decision," says Jared, beaming.

"Good," says JoAnne. "Let's rotate the books. Some of you should bring all the books from the bookshelves, and we'll put out some new books. Let's put out books about all kinds of different families."

Great idea!

Four children race to the book corner, pile up all the books, and stagger to the closet. For the next half hour they sort through the books in the closet, deciding which to bring out and which to leave. *All Kinds of Families* is an easy choice. *Martin's Father, My Mother and I Are Growing Stronger,* and *Two Make a Team,* all of them single parents, are unanimous. But Jared says *The Man Who Didn't Wash Dishes* isn't about a family because the man lives alone. "Lots of people live alone," says JoAnne. "I live alone." "And he has a cat," adds Jorge. Slowly the collection grows: *88 Kisses, Walk Home Tired, Billy Jenkins, My Special Best Words, Is That Your Sister?, Tell Me a Mitzi, Much Bigger Than Martin, Just Us Women.* The title of each selection is read and then decided on. When they have 20 books, they return to the book corner with them and arrange them on the shelves.

When JoAnne imagines her life five years from now, she says, "I won't be teaching. I can't worry about money all the time, and I don't see any way out of it. Perhaps I'll have a bookstore for children. Who knows? I wish people would let us be, let us do what we do well, and stop hassling us about the lights in the room, the rent, and everything else that costs money. But that won't happen, so I'll probably have to leave teaching."

For six years JoAnne has thought about adopting a child, and she has been actively involved in the adoption process for fifteen months. "I'm distracted now because I'm focusing so much energy on adopting a baby. Perhaps when I have a child I'll become re-invested in the day-care center because I'll want my baby to have the same great experience and the sense of community I've helped to give other children." As with so many other choices in her life, JoAnne suffered this decision mightily, weighing the pros and cons, the rewards and the difficulties. Once she decided to go ahead, she met and overcame every obstacle, from lack of money to complicated paperwork. Even though her friends who are single mothers have stressed the difficulty of parenting to her, she is confident that being a single mother by choice sets her apart. "I want to be a parent, to watch my own child grow, to share my love for a lifetime and not just for a few years. It's the next challenge." To make a difference.

On November 2, 1988, JoAnne met her daughter, Dandara Doralise, in a crowded orphanage in Brazil. Dandara was one month old and had been left on the doorstep with a note in Portuguese pinned to her receiving blanket: "I was born October 2. Raise me up." The story of this adoption is a story of bureaucratic insensitivity, outrageous manipulation, financial demands, and questionable ethical practices; it is also a tale of the triumph of compassion when it counted. But all of that is another story. JoAnne and Dandara arrived in New York on November 10 to a tumultuous welcome from friends and community. They were broke and in debt from the trip, but each was enriched in vital ways. Dandara officially enrolled in the day-care center in April. Mother and child are doing fine.

# MICHELE
## What You Teach is Who You Are

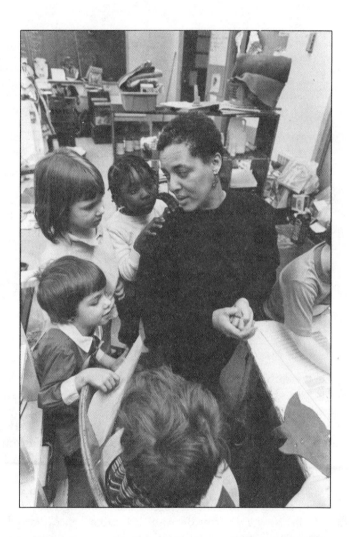

Michele Wilson teaches in a prekindergarten program in an innovative
public elementary school in New York City. She has three daughters, one
in college, one in elementary school, and the youngest in kindergarten.
Michele went to City College, taught in day care for ten years, and has

taught in public school for three years. Her husband teaches in the same school she does, and they share a commitment to urban public education as well as a deep investment in a child-centered approach to teaching. Michele is widely recognized among her peers as an outstanding teacher.

In preparation for a pilot prekindergarten program in New York City, Janice Molnar of the Mayor's Early Childhood Education Commission studied four-year-olds and provided the following unpublished picture of this cohort in 1985: Of 100,000 four-year-olds in New York, 7300 were in Head Start, 10,900 were in Agency for Child Development centers or families, 4100 were in Board of Education prekindergarten programs, and 24,500 were in private day-care centers. These figures add up to 46,800 four-year-olds in some form of preschool care, but that total does not include those in family and home care and so is only a partial description.

Prekindergarten programs could signal the recognition of the importance of quality early childhood programs and of our collective responsibility for their growth and survival. They could also become the occasion to push a regimented, attenuated curriculum inappropriately into the lives of younger children. The question today is not unlike the challenge faced by Head Start more than 20 years ago, a challenge never fully resolved: whether the goal is to hurry young children into the existing educational structures and expected social roles, or whether the movement of families and children into something new and exciting becomes itself a force for building a society where people care more.

North of the fashionable Upper East Side residential and shopping district, just past the huge hospital conglomerate, the sights and sounds take on a distinctly Latin flavor as Madison Avenue becomes Spanish Harlem. Near La Marqueta, the central market that begins on Park Avenue, nestled beneath the elevated railroad tracks before bursting out and sprawling all directions in the open air, an imposing concrete box fills a city block. Its heavy darkness, its grimy barred windows and tall chain-link fences, and its limited crowd-control access all contribute to the sense of an urban institution under siege. This building is, in fact, the brainchild of the New York City Board of Education, an oversized educational complex built twenty-five years ago and currently housing two junior high schools, two elementary schools, and an innovative alternative public school.

At the north end of the building, around a corner and down a winding sidewalk, a playground is filled with the shouts and laughter of twenty-four, four- and five-year-olds chasing and climbing and catching in a whirlwind of color and energy. Their bright scarves and hats and coats are flashes of light as they seem to be blown in all directions. The children are themselves a riot of color, a splash of autumn leaves: light and dark, brown and pink and tan, New York youngsters.

The kids are all vibrant animation, but there is a background, too, that imposes. Rose, a student teacher in this class, wrote in her journal that "the holes in the cyclone fence are adventure to some; one of the stepping places on the climbing tower is missing and the space has become a trash receptacle; and an entire car door has somehow found its way onto the playground. This last item is an attractive artifact and it engages several kids immediately. Andy thinks maybe someone had a wreck here. Eric bets someone brought it here to fix it. José thinks someone lost it." Each idea is considered and discussed as the children whirl over and around their discovery.

The axis of all this vibrating brilliance is a tall 37-year-old woman in an ankle-length dress, overcoat, and oversized scarf. Michele has close-cropped hair that is moving toward salt and pepper, a round and open face, and smiling eyes. Although she never raises her voice above the din and her movements are soft and measured, something about her presence commands attention and exerts an almost gravitational pull on the children. Youngsters appear to fly out to an invisible limit and then orbit back past her, careening and reeling this way and that until they reach the invisible limit in another direction.

In a few minutes it will be lunchtime, and Michele is moving deliberately and unhurriedly to every child or cluster of children, explaining clearly to each that it is nearly time to leave and what to expect next. "We will have to go in for lunch in a few minutes," she repeats several times, "and you will need to put your backpacks on now and begin to get ready." The noise and motion begin to slow—imperceptibly at first—and when Michele finally turns to walk to the school cafeteria, a raggedy but cheerful line of children forms in her wake.

Rose wrote that "the cafeteria scene is a loud and big one, but it probably confused me more than anyone. Michele is hoping that we can use the smaller lunchroom eventually. Sutia mixed her sauerkraut in her peaches and seemed to like the taste." Michele's class is snuggled up at two tables in the far corner of the enormous refectory. The noise is deafening, but the four- and five-year-olds seem oblivious. Several have brought lunches from home, and there is an array of sandwiches, yogurts, fruits, and vegetables; others are eating the school lunch of milk, fish sticks, green beans, bread, and apples, served to them by fifth and sixth graders. There is the concentrated contentment of hungry children eating, and while student teachers, aids, and staff monitor the dining hall, Michele returns to her classroom. Over lunch and straightening up and preparing for the afternoon, Michele offers some insight into her teaching:

"I know that I need to function in some kind of order and organization. I can't be productive with chaos, and I don't think kids can either. The routine, the boundaries, the expectations need to be clear and make some sense to me and to the kids. There's freedom within the organization, and freedom within the control. That sounds funny, but it's true. Once the limits are clear there's a freedom kids can handle."

Her voice has the same calm and deliberate rhythms heard in the playground as she continues. "Especially during transitions, even simple ones like moving from the playground to the cafeteria, young kids can feel threatened and out of control because they're not here and they're not there. What's expected? Where are we? What are the boundaries? It helps if things are clear and laid out. Then we can all see the avenue from here to there, and we can travel along it together. I can see my way, and I hope that the kids can see their ways, too. Of course each child is different. Some kids have no trouble with transitions; they've got a clear sense of themselves and aren't shaken by a little closeness. Some kids become frightened when the boundaries get blurred. And there are some kids who fight the limits. A kid like Ashley fights the control. And yet when she's acting out, flirting, falling apart in anger or confusion or sadness, she's crying out for someone to get control. Once she knows that she's reached the bottom, once she sees that I'll hold fast when she's out of control, she relaxes. She's free to calm down and refocus because I won't let her bounce completely out of control."


Michele's room is at the end of a long corridor behind swinging double doors on the third floor of the sprawling educational complex. The room is really two standard classrooms with the divider pulled back, and it provides generous space for the activities and needs of four- and five-year-olds. The space is a luxury Michele is enjoying, one that allows her to create "my fantasy classroom," but one that she thinks cannot last. "Somewhere the bureaucracy is making different plans," she says with a resigned laugh. "Somewhere powerful forces are negotiating for the 'extra' room." Just the hint of cynicism crosses her face. For now, she is making the most of it.

The room is open and spacious, a room that allows completion of projects, a room for discovery. To the right of the entrance is a large bathroom complete with a toilet, aluminum sink with a wooden crate stepping stool, full-length mirror, and standard-sized bathtub. "We've only used the tub twice, when kids from another classroom got caked with mud, but it's nice to have." To the left are cubbies for coats, lunch boxes, and backpacks. In the center of the room is a large library area defined by movable chest-high bookshelves, a rug, and carpet squares for sitting. There is a listening area with record player, books, and earphones; a writing and drawing space; an animal study area with guinea pigs in cages; and a space for math games and puzzles. Behind a waist-high partition in the far corner is a complete kitchen with ample storage and counter space, stove, oven, and refrigerator. Low tables and chairs in each area complete the scene. "The room asks you to walk, not charge," says Michele. "And hopefully it invites you into areas that are large and well-defined enough so that a child can feel, for example, separated and quiet for reading, and yet I can stand almost anywhere and see the whole."

The adjoining room has four large sinks, a sand area, a water table, an art table for working with clay and making collages, a double easel for painting, a sewing table, a playhouse, and a block-building area that takes up over a third of the space. Michele has put a sign in each area indicating the number of people who can work or play there; for example, "Listening Area/2 People" is followed by an outline sketch of two children. "This is an example of freedom within the organization," Michele explains. "Three people would ruin the listening area for everyone, but with two they are free to explore, experiment, and learn."

The walls of Michele's room are filled with a rainbow of children's artwork as well as a range of homemade charts and graphs and surveys. One poster-sized sheet of newsprint asks, "Do you like raisins?" Down the left side of the paper is each child's name, and to the right a large "YES" and "NO." Different colored lines are drawn from each name to the appropriate answer. The "NO" stands virtually alone, while the "YES" is a scramble of colored lines. Another survey asks, "Do you like peanut butter?" A "YES" column and a "NO" column each are followed by a series of checks, each check signifying a child in the class. And a third asks, "Which crackers do you like?" There is a picture of a stoned-wheat cracker and a picture of a Triscuit, and underneath each are glued small pieces of paper, each piece indicating a child's preference (stoned-wheat wins easily).

Since this is Michele's "fantasy classroom," it is important to know what she had in mind when she chose to set it up as she did.

"I wanted the block area in the other room because I wanted uninterrupted space and a place where the noise of building wouldn't be disruptive. The block area is the most important area in my classroom and I wanted that space to reflect that. That far-away area, long and tremendous, said blocks to me when I first saw it." One long wall is lined with low shelves filled with wooden blocks of different sizes and shapes. Taped to each shelf is a black silhouette drawn on white cardboard showing the length and shape of a particular block. During clean-up, children can find the appropriate shelf for the units, the double units, the half units, the cylinders, the ramps, and so on.

"Blocks are a favorite material of mine," Michele continues. "I like their solidity, their feel. I like to see kids discover what they can do with blocks, and that involves discovering the limitations of blocks, too. For example, you can't mold blocks and you can't change their shape. Learning about the limits of blocks opens up enormous possibilities for expression and fantasy and play."

As she warms to the discussion of blocks, her hands become animated and underline her points. "Blocks are of central importance because of all the possibilities, the way block building touches on so many other areas. Language development, for example. When kids build with blocks they talk. They describe what they're doing and what they're thinking. They extend what they know through their play and they talk as they do it. They find words to fit what they're doing, and it feeds off of itself and grows. Some kids want labels or signs for their buildings, and these kids come to writing through blocks. Sometimes they dictate or write stories about their buildings. In all these ways language is part of block building.

"Another area is mathematics. Building with blocks is an extended math lesson, but it's practical problem-solving math with a concrete purpose, not math as abstractions. For example, block builders know about addition and subtraction, fractions and equivalence, but they know these things in their fingertips simply from repeatedly making a city or a building. They have to deal all of the time with problems like two of a certain block equaling one of another, or of bridging a certain space with a particular block. One group of kids I had spent weeks figuring out the mechanics of ramps on bridges because their toy cars had wheels and they wanted to get them onto the bridges the proper way. We went to the George Washington Bridge and walked the span, and that helped enormously. They finally solved the problem and had these magnificent bridges with staircases for people and curving ramps for cars. That was phenomenal to watch."

Next to the block area is an area that invites dress-up and dramatic play. There are dolls and cradles, hats and vests, pieces of material, and adult shoes. "I wanted that kind of play to go along with the block building," Michele explains. "Block play is one way children work out their thinking and feelings in a public, concrete way. Adults tend to work these things out in conversation or discussion, while kids are more body-oriented. Fantasy or dramatic play is another way children interpret experiences and make them their own. So the two areas complement one another."

The library/reading area is the dominant space in the first room, with writing and listening areas, for example, as satellites to it. "I wanted the library central to the room because books are important to me and books need to become important to them," Michele explains. "I wanted the space to say to kids that books are important. I wanted to surround them with books. All kinds, all sizes. I also wanted a meeting place large enough for the whole group to sit and be comfortable, even to stretch and relax."

The kitchen, which occupies a large corner of the room, is a hub of activity most mornings. "I didn't choose the kitchen," Michele says, "but if I could have, I would have. Even in rooms where I didn't have a functioning kitchen I did cooking with kids—'cool' cooking or cooking without heat, things like peanut butter balls and fruit salads. Cooking with kids is another example of something that incorporates so many things naturally into an activity that is both fun and worthwhile in its own right. Cooking draws together language, reading, math, science, and social studies in a completely organic way. So I try to cook every day, and as much as possible I want the kids to develop an ability to cook things themselves. I have a set format for recipes, which they learn and which they themselves can follow. They can see from the drawings, for example, that two cups of flour go into the bowl and get mixed together with the six tablespoons of butter and a cup of sugar, and so on. In a sense they're reading the recipe, measuring and mixing, creating."

The kids return from lunch with a rush of noise and energy. Michele greets them and helps them organize their things in the cubbies and then get settled down. She quietly reads a book to the whole group in the library and then asks children to pick the area of the room they want to work in. The process is slow and deliberate. Blocks is a popular choice and fills up quickly, followed by sewing and stuffing doll-like guinea pigs at the art table, then the dramatic play area and the listening area. Eventually each child is busy at something, and Michele and her student teachers begin to circulate to each area to check in and to help if necessary. As she passes Rose, who is working with the children who are sewing, she comments on the calm, purposefulness of the moment, whispering, "This is how it's supposed to be."

The block area is alive with a large farm encompassed by a corral and including stables, crops, and machinery; an enormous airplane in which its two builders and pilots sit; and a construction site where José, wearing a hard hat, supervises the imaginary pouring of cement: José is at the same time in the construction site working and outside of it directing what the little wooden figures are doing, and he moves effortlessly from one perspective to the other.

In the playhouse three girls are cooking eggs. One boy from the block area reaches in to borrow the phone: "Hello. Mama, I need you," he says, and hangs up.

Michele stops at the listening area. "This is *Caps for Sale*," she says to Sasha. "Where's the *Caps for Sale* book that goes with this? Remember you have to put the record with the book and put it back on the shelf before you begin the next one. Okay, now you can begin *The Wild Swans*."

Ashley is making a bold, bright painting at the easel. Larina comments derisively, "She's painting what she did yesterday."

Michele says, "That's all right. Some children like to paint the same picture several times." Michele's voice is not scolding but affirming, explaining, direct. It remains soft and expressive, without a hint of impatience, strain, or patronizing. Even in a situation that contains built-in contradictions, her manner and her tone are matter-of-fact. "You didn't finish picking up the Play-Doh," she says to Alexander, Andy, and David, who are gleefully gluing paper at the art table. "Go and finish. And remember it needs to be in one big ball." The three race off and are back in a flash. Michele covers the glue container with her hand and adds, "One more thing. The Play-Doh table needs to be wiped." They jump up again and are gone. Perhaps these are particularly agreeable four-year-olds, or perhaps the fact that Michele's voice and manner are so straightforward and peaceful mediates against tension and conflict. Again and again she affirms, acknowledges, and understands, even as she interacts and participates. Again and again the children respond.

At one point Annika comes to Michele looking sour and scrunched up, whining, "Michele, Ashley stepped on my finger."

"That must have hurt. Did you tell Ashley?"

"No."

"Well, you need to tell Ashley."

Michele goes with Annika to Ashley and says, "Ashley, you stepped on Annika's finger and that hurt her. If it was an accident, would you please tell Annika you're sorry?"

Ashley looks cloudy and heavy but she leans her head toward Michele's face and murmurs. In a moment Michele turns to Annika and says, "She said she's sorry—very softly."

Ashley presents a particular challenge to Michele because she is the first child Michele has taught who has Down's Syndrome. "It's an experiment," Michele explains later. "Sometimes I think it's not going to work because the demands of the classroom are too great. Other times I think it will work, and everyone will benefit. I don't know. I'm just learning."

Ashley's parents wanted her mainstreamed in a public school classroom, and they have worked out a special arrangement with the school, which allows Ashley to attend Michele's class provided there is an aide to work with Ashley in class and to stay involved with the school in monitoring and assessing Ashley's progress. This arrangement creates difficulties for Michele.

"Having an aide in this situation is a mixed blessing," she explains. "On the one hand, it's another adult to help in the room. On the other hand, that gives me another person to supervise. So I'm in the position of figuring out how to work with Ashley, training the aide to do that too, supervising her work with others in the classroom, and so on. Furthermore, Ashley can be so disruptive that she more than offsets the extra pair of hands. So it's a struggle."

Rose wrote an entry in her journal early in the year: "Ashley's Dad stayed with her today. She seemed calmer, but he seemed too persistent—and rather self-conscious about Ashley's behavior . . . he was trying to force her to sit in a chair at snack time . . . I think it was uncomfortable for everyone to watch him hold her tightly and try to force her into the chair. It was as if he were trying to make her be 'normal.' But, of course, he knows her and has lived with this for a long time. His is not an easy load to bear."

When Michele wanted to explain to the class about Down's Syndrome, Ashley's father worried that the children were too young to understand. Michele felt that they needed some straightforward explanation and sent a note to the other children's parents explaining Down's Syndrome and urging them to use that correct term instead of "sick" or "bad" as some of them had been using. Michele did talk openly with the children about Ashley in the hope of helping her and the other children to understand and accept her special differentness. "Ashley works more slowly," Michele began. "You all know that. Some days she says 'I can't sew.' But Friday Ashley finished her guinea pig. It took her longer." Then Michele read a book someone had made for Ashley called "A Story About Daisy." The simple illustrations are of an adorable and approachable child with Down's Syndrome who has an open face with wide-apart eyes and a crooked smile.

"This is Daisy. She likes to dress up. She likes to play with her friends.

She likes to look in the mirror. But sometimes Daisy's friends go too fast and climb too high and talk in grown-up ways that Daisy doesn't understand. Then Daisy is alone with her doll. Daisy's Mommy picks her up. Mommy says, 'I know things are hard for you sometimes. That's because you have Down's Syndrome. That means you learn and grow slower. Sometimes things go too fast. Sometimes it helps to take a rest.' Daisy rests with Mommy. She looks at her doll. 'You have Down's Syndrome,' she tells her baby doll. 'You grow slowly.' The baby doll looked like she wanted to take a walk. Daisy took her baby doll for a walk. She heard her friend Jane yell, 'Wait for me!' They walked together."

The children listened with rapt attention. Ashley looked at the book and then looked at the children near her. She untied her shoes and rolled over. When Michele finished, Katie said, "On May 18 I'll be five." José said, "I don't want any more books." And when Xavier said, "I want the book," Ashley said in a firm voice, "No, it's my book." Michele said, "Yes, it's your book, and it's about Down's Syndrome and a child who learns more slowly."

"It may work out with Ashley," Michele says later. "Sometimes I see her using an area of the room the way I'd planned for it to be used, or I see her respond to something simple and direct, and I get goosebumps. We'll see."

Michele plans her days carefully, and each day is an intricate dance of patterns and improvisation, regular routines and specific, individual needs. She begins most mornings with writing time. Children are organized into writing groups of from four to eight and assigned to specific tables. Sometimes Michele suggests a topic for writing, based, for example, on a trip or some other shared experience, but often she simply provides the space and materials for writing. The room takes on a quiet, purposeful tone as 24 children work with pencil and markers on pages Michele has stapled together into personalized books. "This started when I was in day care and I had a small group one year who were particularly enthusiastic about dictating stories," Michele explains. "I saw the value for everyone, and it evolved into something I do with all kids every year." Later, when I asked Michele to write down a few early positive memories, she wrote: "Sitting at the dining room table as my mother worked behind me in the kitchen. I was writing letters, all the letters I knew. My sister—two-and-a half years older—was at school. I turned around and asked my mother, 'How do you spell my name?' I wrote as she told me. I looked at it and it was mine."

These children are mainly drawing pictures and then calling one or another adult over who can take down dictation. Some of the dictation is simply labeling: "This is food. This is a dog." Some of the children dictate elaborate stories. Some write their own names on the paper, while a few make first attempts at inventive spelling, such as: "Sentrul Park." "The important thing," explains Michele, "is that kids see their own words and thoughts validated. Reading and writing can emerge organically if opportunities for self-expression occur in a word-rich environment."

Sometimes words and pictures interact in a way that they build on each other. José says, "This is a man," and then stops to add something to the picture, explaining, "I forgot his eyebrows." One day, Sutia changed the subject of her story as she spoke: "This is about a car. Purple and red. Red and yellow. This is about flowers." Sutia's picture on this day was an intricate color and line design with no identifiable representational figures, but with an elaborate accompanying story: "The brown went to our house. The blue and the black went to the purple. Can you be my lover, purple? He went to the red. The red and the green went to the purple. Purple, purple, can you be my lover?"

Melia is five and insists on struggling to write her own words. Her writing is functional, not fanciful, and is full of letters and surveys and declarations: "I have to look after the baby all the time." Her book contains a series of letters to Michele: "Dear Michele. I love you. This is a witch hat on Michele." "This is Michele. I love Michele. Can I spend the night with Michele?" "Dear Michele. I love you forever. Even if you be buried I still love you."

Michele tells Max she is ready to write his words. Max begins, "This is the water." Michael rushes up and says he needs words. Michele asks him to wait until she's finished with Max's words. Max continues, "This is the train. This is the controls." Michele asks, "Is this the train that is underground or the train that goes over the river?" Max clarifies the picture, "This is the train over here and this is the tram." He finishes, "This is the grass and people are running in the grass."

After writing time, six children help set up snack while the rest of the group reads a story. Setting up snack is complicated for four- and five-year-olds and Michele allows space and an ample time for them to work on it. Nicole keeps counting to eight, but she is not matching one cup and one napkin with each other. It takes her several attempts to get eight cups and eight napkins in front of eight chairs. She then goes to the kitchen and puts 16 crackers in a basket and takes it to her table. After all the tables are organized, each snack helper takes a turn selecting the appropriate number of classmates for her or his table. "It's time-consuming and messy doing snack this way," says Michele, "but there's measurable growth in competence and skill in just a few weeks, and the sense of purpose and accomplishment is wonderful. Besides, this is the curriculum. No sense rushing when this is exactly where we're going."

After snack is cleaned up, the whole group gathers for Meeting in the library before work time. This is a time when rules and routines can be reviewed, important information disseminated, exciting events shared together. It was at Meeting that Michele's class met the visiting Panamanian children who had danced in the all-school assembly one day. It was at Meeting that Michele introduced the gerbils to the children, and José kept calling them rats, and Max worried that the daddy was dead (his father died when Max was two). It was at Meeting that the children named the hamster; and took a survey about who likes cheese, placing a wooden peg in a "YES" column or a "NO" column, and then discussed "more than" and "less than," and used the survey as a way of voting for snack food. It was at Meeting that the group decided to keep the jack-o'-lanterns and observe them every day for weeks as they rotted. Rose noted in her journal the content of one important Meeting: "Michele wrote a story today with the class about a seed growing. She showed them seeds at different stages, and wrote and drew pictures about the process on a large sheet of newsprint everyone could see. We had some squirmers, but there were lots of very interested expressions. We've had lots of seeds sprouting from the kids' planting projects—popcorn, kidney beans, lima beans, sunflower seeds, pumpkin seeds."

Michele wants her classroom to nurture life, human life but also plant and animal life. Her room feels alive with noise, with color, with smell, and with activity. Reflecting on the importance of plants and animals Michele comments, "I grew up in the [housing] projects and so cats and dogs weren't allowed but we always had parakeets, turtles, fish, hamsters. My father had wanted to be a veterinarian. The interest in animals came from him, and he encouraged it in us. He was always trying something new, changing their environments, teaching them things, studying them. We all picked it up from him. We had loads of plants at home, which were my father's also. He and I replanted and propagated plants together twice a year. We never had a garden though—no space."

How does Michele account for the teacher she has become? How does she understand her pathway to teaching? In many ways her road to teaching is as direct and straightforward as the woman herself.

"I'm a New York product through and through," she begins. "I was born in Bellevue Hospital in 1949, grew up on the Lower East Side, attended P. S. 34 and Junior High School 60, graduated from Washington Irving High School in 1967 and City College in 1974, where I also got a master's degree in 1984. I haven't really gone very far," she says with an ironic laugh. "I still live in Manhattan and it's the place I know best."

Michele's map of her pathway to teaching has roots that run to the South. "My folks met in New Jersey during the Second World War, but both were raised in Virginia. My Mom was a nurse and Dad a subway motorman. They were both honest, hard-working people, and both had the southern-black passion for education. To them an education was crucial, something valuable in itself, and something no one could take away from you once you got it. I grew up in a context that esteemed education. In my family, TEACHER is spelled with capital letters. I remember my aunt working to integrate the schools in Prince Georges County, and later coming to New York because it was not safe for her in Virginia. She recently got her Ph.D., and that was held up in our family as an example of the most highly prized success."

Recalling her own earliest school experience, Michele remembers an intense feeling that not knowing how to tie her own shoes in school would present her with a serious barrier or embarrassment. She asked her Dad to teach her, and she remembers the deep satisfaction she felt going to school that first day knowing how to tie her own shoes.

"There were only a few black kids in P. S. 34 in the 1950s," she continues. "The Lower East Side was changing then. It was Jewish and Italian and Irish, and blacks and Puerto Ricans were just coming in. I remember the first Puerto Rican kid in my class. There was only one black teacher, Viola Harper, and she was my fifth-grade teacher. She was special. She did a lot of things other teachers didn't do, like taking us to Rockefeller Center for ice skating." Interestingly, Michele now takes her class ice skating every Friday, an activity the children find challenging but fun. "Miss Harper was strict, but she could be fun-loving underneath her no-nonsense exterior. We knew she liked us, and she thought we could *do*. We all knew that, but I think she especially took care of the black kids, a mission I feel I continue in my work today because all schools—even the best ones—are tracked, and even in good schools racism exists in subtle forms and the contradictions can be profound. It's hard to confront racism when everyone denies its existence and skirts the issue. Miss Harper was different. She fought the system in a quiet way. She fought for kids to make it. So in the fifth grade I decided to become a teacher. There were no chance factors involved, no accidents of fate. It was as deliberate and planned as anything can be, and I pursued it right up to the present. School was my job, and I could see doing that as an adult. I liked the idea of being as important to people as Miss Harper was to me. I still feel her presence resonating in me in the ways I try to get kids to feel capable and in the no-nonsense way I organize the class."

In mapping her own pathway to teaching, she draws a great solid line dividing the paper in two, a line representing the birth of her first child in 1970. She describes that solid line as a "turnaround point. I always knew I wanted to teach, but when Sharis was born I knew whom to teach—her—and where to teach—group day care."

Family is an important theme to Michele—the family she grew up in and the family she is raising. These families, of course, overlap and resonate in her teaching. "One thing I learned from my family long ago that continues to be important in my teaching is the gentle tension between the needs of individuals and the needs of a group. In my family each person got the fullest support to do his or her own thing, but each had a responsibility to the family. There are certain things in my family you can't do, like you can't hurt yourself with drugs, you can't drop out, you can't fail to take care of the people who depend on you. You can be anything and everything you are, but it has to be in a social context, a constructive, whole, and decent context. The message is that you'll be supported all the way, but you can't tear yourself or anyone else apart. In teaching, this is always a tension, and I remember the fierce directness with which my family approached it. I see each kid as an individual, and I try to help them to see each other as distinct and unique. At the same time we are a group, a community, and we have social goals that are necessary and important. So each is free to grow and to be, but each must also grow to see the whole. I guess that's why I find that I like a lot of kids whom other teachers find challenging or impossible. I like kids who struggle for who they are, kids for whom life is not all given. I like eccentric kids, kids who are their own persons, kids with a sense of self and others. Kids who give me trouble are the self-involved kids who can't get past their own skin and who find life on a platter."

Later, when asked to write a vignette about a child who is rewarding to work with, Michele drew a sketch of Kristopher: "I don't know Kristopher very well. I know that he absolutely loves 'his school' and derives great satisfaction from his experiences in class. He lives a rich internal life. He literally moves and dances to music only he hears, tells himself stories, gets lost in textural experiences. He has good sturdy relationships with other kids. Kristopher is four, and part of the joy and reward of working with him is knowing I've got another year to be with him and watch who he is unfold."

By contrast, Janet is particularly unrewarding: "She won't invest herself in anything. She hangs back, chipping away, picking things apart. She won't try to change things, nor will she accept things and make a go of it. She whines, complains, yet is deeply passive as if things should change for her. Ugh!"

When Michele was first teaching, her oldest daughter attended City and Country School. "Sharis had an extraordinary teacher at City and Country named Virginia Parker. Virginia understood kids as well as anyone I've ever seen. She listened carefully and always responded to a question with another question, not in a gimmicky way but in a serious way, something I was in awe of and have never fully mastered in my own teaching. Virginia never raised her voice, was never gung-ho and overpowering, but she was engaged with children's minds and they knew it. I studied Virginia, and I've tried to be like her in those ways."

Michele learned from other teachers as well. "I loved Carol Mulligan's enjoyment of teaching, her passion, and her visceral pleasure in the act itself. I loved walking into her room because it was full of life and surprise. I also admired her commitment to public education for black children, for poor and working-class kids. When I took her job here, she went to a wreck of a school in a defeated neighborhood because, she said, 'These kids here don't need me.' "

Michele notes that her three strongest model teachers are black women. "We tend to be overlooked and unsung, you know, often assumed to be incapable of teaching our own or knowing how to raise our own. I've never seen any better than these three heroic, master teachers, each a black woman, and yet I've never seen them held up as models in all the discussion of education, either."

Michele's formal teacher education took place at City College before the time of Lillian Weber and the Workshop Center for Open Education. "I went to City when it was called the 'proletariat Harvard' and it was for smart white kids. Blacks were a tiny, though vocal, minority on campus. I was the only black person in most of my classes, and I was pregnant."

Teacher education was patronizing and oppressive at City. The underlying sense was that teaching was an easy career choice, mainly for women, or, if it had any higher meaning, it was to save the less fortunate. There was no vision of teaching as part of creating a better society, and there was no sense of helping people understand the realities of teaching or the lives of children. "It was a difficult and demoralizing time for me," Michele remembers.

She feels fortunate, though, to have student taught in a nursery school where she saw people coming to teaching through knowing and respecting children and being genuinely invested in their lives. For the next 10 years she taught in a city day-care center that allowed her to teach as she chose to teach, and she blossomed. "Before I began there, the director told me, 'Don't worry about the rest of it, the rest of it they'll get from books. What you teach is who you are.' I've held on to that, and it's been a central teaching idea for me from the beginning. I try to be myself, exactly who I am as a person. I want kids to know me as an individual, to know what I value, and to know by the way I am and the way I talk to them that they are of the utmost importance."

Asked to describe success in her work, Michele speaks of "the productive hum when children are actively engaged with each other" and "when kids struggle through a difficult problem and are aware that they are doing it." She goes on to explain that being a teacher is what she enjoys most about life. "There's no separation between me as teacher; me, mother; me, wife; me, sister; and me, Michele. Being one influences and enriches all the others.

"What I like best about teaching is seeing kids puzzled, engaged, and challenged. There's a certain intense look that goes with this, and a look of satisfaction that can follow that puts me on a cloud. It can happen to whole groups of kids or to individuals working alone. That's the reward of teaching for me. There's also a satisfaction at being in on the beginning of things and of having kids come back and say, 'This was the best.' I look at older kids and think that so much is already settled. I like the little ones."

Asked what she would change in teaching, Michele says, "Numbers and money. There's always too many kids and always too few resources. But I don't dwell on it because for a lot of people those realities become a cop-out from doing the best they can. There's always a job that can be done, but that's what I'd change. And I'd change the perception of day care and early childhood education generally. Magically, I'd make everyone understand what I do, that it's critically important and potentially of enormous value to kids and families and all of society."

Michele wants to teach for several more years, but someday she imagines living outside of the country. When her own three children are grown, she dreams of going to Brazil or West Africa. "Africa, because it's my cultural source and because it's in a state of tremendous political and social change that I'd like to witness and experience. Brazil, for similar reasons and because it's part of the new world. I've heard that in Brazil people genuinely don't see the color of a person's skin. I also love the language and the music. Perhaps I'll find other lives and other things to do."

When I gave Michele a copy of what I'd written, her reaction was mixed. "There are things I like about it. I like being seen in such a positive light. But there's also something unreal. I'm not that good, and you know it. You never show me when I've lost it and am going up the walls."

I point out to her that I have never seen her "going up the walls" in all the days I have spent in her classroom. She laughs and shrugs. "Maybe I'm on my best behavior when I see you come through that door."

Michele conveys a sense of incompleteness, a sense of reaching, of going beyond, which is perhaps lost in this portrait. For example, when asked to list the adjectives that best describe her as a teacher, Michele included four that would have been on my list and a fifth that was a surprise: nurturing, stimulating, calm, quiet, unsatisfied. She strives for something more. Similarly, when creating an image of her teaching with clay, she shaped and reshaped the clay, never stopping; when asked to describe it, she said, "Well, it's flat now with little bumps, and it's changing and growing, now it's round and getting longer." Her hands kept working; she never settled on a single object to hold up as her image.

Later she wrote, "It's true that I project calm and patience into my teaching, and that has something to do with how kids learn. I've become more able to support children as they initiate and sustain their own growth and learning. I'm more attentive to the ways children think and make sense of the world, I'm more sensitive to their quest, and therefore I'm better at what I do. At the same time I find that I feel an even more urgent need to 'perfect' the classroom, to make it more nurturing and more stimulating simultaneously, an environment that supports and encourages inquiry."

Michele's teaching, beautiful in itself, is also inspiring for what it is not yet.

Michele has had a good class this year, she reports. It's been a stellar year for her family as well. Her youngest child, Jamilya, is playing the violin and beginning to read. Micco, her second, is finally a comfortable reader and "runs the school, by all accounts." Michele says that the triumph of this year is that Sharis has come through her first year in college in very nice shape. "Sharis and I are becoming friends on a more adult level, and that's kind of nice. She also missed Micco and Jamilya in a real way and is more loving and caring than ever. It's been a very good year."

# ⭐ 6 ⭐

# DARLENE
## Witness to the Unimaginable

Darlene Mosley began teaching in day care in 1978 and has been director or head teacher in several settings. She is married and the mother of four children, two boys and two girls. Besides teaching and parenting, Darlene is a graduate student in educational administration and special education. She is well known and highly regarded among early childhood professionals.

While women joining the waged labor force could represent a de-mocratizing and progressive trend, in reality this has not happened. The entry of women into the work force has not been matched by any shar-ing of their traditional labor, domestic work and child care, which has resulted in a double-shift for most working women. Further, the 55 per-cent of American women in the work force, still earn, on average, 59 cents for every dollar earned by men. Women in the waged work force are often part of the huge army of unemployed or marginal workers. Furthermore, unemployment rates for black women are twice those for whites, and Third World teen-age women are the most severely unem-ployed group in society.

Poverty has a disproportionate impact on women and children. Three-quarters of those who became poor between 1979 and 1983 were either children, or adults with dependents. Of the 35 million poor people in this country, over 13 million are children, which amounts to one in every five children. Added to this is the growing Dickensian nightmare of homelessness. Forty percent of the homeless nationwide are chil-dren. Of the 11,000 homeless children in New York, 5000 are under five. And yet only 10 percent of all homeless families in emergency housing participate in formal child-care arrangements.

Of course, reading the statistics on poverty and homelessness has become commonplace, and we can begin to look without seeing. The injustice of it is acknowledged even as we adjust out gaze. Perhaps we have each accustomed ourselves to the familiar bag lady or beggar in the doorway. But poverty and homelessness are not natural disasters; they are the result of the actions of people. As we look at the growing crisis of homeless families, we must remember that whatever human beings construct, they can also deconstruct and reconstruct. With enough thought we can understand our situations, and with enough commitment we can change them.

The front room is alive with activity. David and Maurice are building a runway with wooden blocks. Darlene, their teacher, sits in the middle of the block pile offering support and assistance. "Beautiful, David. It's going really well. Here, Maurice, use this big one, get some more of the long ones from over there."

David and Maurice are intent on building the longest runway they can make. Carl comes and joins them, but they hardly notice. Their attention is on the task at hand. Shaquan and Ebony occupy a small block building in one corner where they seem to be putting dolls to bed and then waking them up. "This is my hotel," says Ebony. "And it's only for me and my friends."

Maurice pushes a perilously high stack of long blocks slowly across the room toward the runway. Just as it arrives at its destination, it crashes loudly to the floor, and David laughs and rushes up to untangle the wreckage and keep the runway going.

The room has barred windows and walls covered with brightly colored murals. "I did these with the kids when the center opened," Darlene explains. "Some of them are nice, but they're a bit too permanent. Now I want to put the kids' art work up and I can't. Soon I think I'll repaint the walls."

The murals are done in big sections, each dominated by the outline of a child. Each child's outline is filled in with paint, some haphazard and gaudy, others more representational. "You should have seen us working on this project," Darlene smiles enthusiastically. "I traced each kid's body outline on big sheets of paper on the floor. Some couldn't stop giggling lying there, the center of so much work and attention. Then I retraced the outlines on the wall and set the kids up with smocks and paint. It was wild in a wonderful kind of way. Some kids worked on it for the longest time. Well, you can see the results."

The large front room is connected to a smaller room with child-size tables and chairs, a patch of rug, closets, and shelves for materials and books. There is a fish tank, a sand table, cubbies, and a small kitchen area in one corner. Darlene's colleague and assistant, Marilyn, is sitting at the table with Natika, Afrinique, and Pete, gluing bits of colored paper, cut material, and photos from newspapers onto large pieces of cardboard. "Teacher," Pete wails. "Someone took my glue."

"Doesn't everyone have a cup?" Marilyn asks.

"Yea, but she dipped in mine."

"Okay, Natika. This is yours. And Pete, there's more if you run out." Changing directions, she asks, "Doesn't glue feel funny on your fingers?"

Pete frowns and says, "It's yukky." Afrinique dips her whole hand in the glue and, watching the thick white drops fall back into the cup, smiles contentedly.

Darlene tells the runway builders that everyone is going to clean up in five minutes. "Lee, go and tell Marilyn we're having Circle in five minutes." Lee runs off and the business of picking up and putting away begins. Shaquan is picking up in the dress-up area, and as Darlene passes, she looks up and says casually, "Teacher, I'm drunk! This orange juice has something in it." "What's drunk?" Darlene asks, matching Shaquan's casualness, somewhere between teasing and probing.

"That's when you cry and yell and moan. When Heather's drunk she yells."

"Okay, but the juice is fine, and we're not going to yell or moan or be drunk here. Okay? Finish picking up." Shaquan goes back to the task at hand.

Soon the blocks and cars and dress-ups and dolls are all resting in their places. The children from the other room join the rest of the group in a circle on the floor. Trina, tiny for a four-year-old, cuddles into Marilyn's lap and sobs softly. She never speaks and is never far from Marilyn.

Darlene pulls a child-sized chair and a portable easel with a large sheet of paper clipped to it into the circle, sits down, and begins, "Yesterday was Wednesday. Remember what we did? We played here, and then some of us went on a long trip to the river."

"It was hot, too."

"It was far."

"I like the park."

"Okay," Darlene continues. "Yesterday was Wednesday and today is Thursday."

"Thursday," Kenny echoes.

Darlene writes "Today is Thursday" in big letters on the top of the paper with a black marker. "How does it look outside?"

"Hot!" say nine voices in unison.

"Hot," Darlene agrees, and she writes "Today it looks hot," adding a quick yellow picture of a smiling sun.

"Who wants to tell me what you did today?"

"Me!" says David. "Me and Maurice made a long runway. It was for planes."

"Did everyone see David and Maurice's runway?" Darlene asks as she jots down their names and what they did. "We left it up and some of you can play with it after snack."

"Who else wants to tell me what you did?"

"I sprayed water on Kenny," says Pete, bragging. "I got him wet."

"And what are the rules of the water table?" Darlene asks, serious but not punishing.

"No spraying!" Pete shouts. Darlene writes down "Pete—Sprayed Kenny with water, but knows better."

Ebony says "I played with water, too."

"What else?"

"I made a picture."

"Okay, Ebony made a beautiful collage," Darlene says as she writes.

After everyone has had a chance to share an activity—"I made tea," "I put a hat on my doll," "I cried"—Darlene pushes the easel aside and leans forward slowly, conspiratorially looking mysteriously from face to face. The kids lean in ever so slightly too, wondering what's next. "Guys" she says, almost whispering, "Guys, you are so good and so important I brought a surprise for you from my house."

Pete shouts, "Let's see!" and the group erupts in shouts and pleas. They leap up to crowd around Darlene as she rummages in a big, dark, carrying bag. Triumphantly she pulls a large, gray rock from the bag.

"This," she says, holding it up for all to see, "is for the fish tank." "Ohhh!" the kids shout, and each wants a turn holding the large, gray rock. Maurice inspects it carefully, turning it over a few times in his hands; Natika holds it carefully too, like gold.

"There's more," Darlene says more briskly. "Here's a larger pump for the tank so it will stay cleaner, and here's some plants for the bottom." Darlene holds up the materials for the tank and then gathers them under her chair while the rock continues to be passed around. "After snack some of you can work with me on cleaning the fish tank."

Soon the children are singing as a group: a naming song around the whole circle, a counting song, a song about freedom, and a jumping song. After the jumping song, Darlene leads them in a little exercise routine:

"Okay, stand on one foot. Now the other. Good. Now walk backward. Jump forward! Now backward. Now do jumping-jack-and-jills. Okay, now fall down! Now take five deep breaths. Okay, close your eyes. Relax . . . Relax. . . ."

When all is quiet, she says in a soft voice, "Let's have snack now," and the children scramble to the table. Snack today is crackers and bananas and juice. Everyone eats except Trina, who is still sobbing, but quietly, inside herself. Her hands are dirty, and her fingernails are broken.

"I don't know Trina well yet," Darlene says later. "She's been coming here for about three weeks, but she's never said a word and never changed expression. She stays close to Marilyn and that's good. But I really can't get much from her or her Mom."

Darlene is the director of a day-care center for homeless children. Most of them have never known life outside of a hotel, and many have lived on the street or have migrated from shelter to shelter. All of them have known hunger, fear, and violence.

"This is an important program," Darlene says. "It's small, of course, and nowhere near adequate to the need, but it's important." Darlene's center is on the first floor of a formerly abandoned building. The building has been rehabilitated, and upstairs are eight furnished apartments. Homeless families occupy the apartments on a temporary basis, while a social service staff works with each to solve problems and find employment, health care, and affordable housing for them. Once members of a family are organized and their condition is minimally improved, they move on to new homes, and another homeless family takes their place. For the months or years they are in transition and living in the building, Darlene takes care of their preschool-age children.

"These kids are special," Darlene asserts. "They show you how resilient kids can be. Look at Maurice. He's so sturdy in many ways. But they also show you how damaging it is to be hurt. Not hurt once, but hurt again and again. Some days working with these kids can fill you with joy and you have such faith in people's spirits. Other days you just want to cry."

Darlene works a lot with parents. "A lot of the women are angry, of course," she says. "And it's not easy. I try to build up a sense of trust first. They're supposed to fill out a lot of forms, but I try not to start with that. I try to start with a kind word or just talk about the kids."

She continues, "Of course, for folks whose lives are out of control it can be kind of touchy. Maybe the only place they feel in control is with their own kids. And not being able to provide even the basics to their kids is taking a toll. I try to push gently about the kids. How important it is to cuddle them and have time for them without the TV. That kind of thing. I try to get the parents in here, to make a link between home and school. I try to teach them and teach the kids."

Darlene has taught for more than 10 years. "I always knew I would be a teacher because I always knew I had something to share. I toyed with being a nurse for awhile, or a social worker. But teaching was my choice from a very young age. I just knew."

Darlene went to City College, in New York City where she was influenced by Lillian Weber and the Workshop Center for Open Education. She learned about how to organize environments that allowed children to take the initiative in their own learning. She learned how to plan for child-centered activities and how to stimulate a sense of sharing and mutual respect. "Open education is harder," she says now, "because it demands so much of you. You have to be tuned in to kids, responsive, and always on. I had no idea teaching would involve all that it does, but I wouldn't change it."

Darlene describes her own four children as the "center of my life." In a dog-eared snapshot propped up on a crowded bookshelf, the children stand erect, unsmiling in front of Darlene and her tall, broad-shouldered, full-bearded husband. Everyone's eyes are fixed directly, unflinchingly on the camera. Darlene rests one hand on her husband's arm, the other on her oldest son's shoulder. They look regal.

Darlene's family emigrated from St. Thomas to New York, where she was born. She lived part of her childhood with her grandmother in the Caribbean and remembers it as difficult and harsh. "It was basic survival, a lot of work," she says. "I sometimes wonder if I'd be a different person today if I'd had the kind of mothering I give to my kids. I'm happy now, but I still wonder how my life might have been different."

Darlene is also deeply involved in her Christian faith. "I'm passionate about everything I do," she says, "and so I study the Bible passionately too. It's a historic and inspired book. The chaos and turmoil of this world has turned me toward the Bible. I worry about the callousness all around me, the stressfulness and the callousness. Religion and family provide a home for me."

Somehow Darlene finds time for family, work, religion, and some extras as well. Sometimes she makes space to go to a nearby hospital to cuddle the boarder babies, that is, those who live there. "They need human contact so much," she says. "They're not responsible for what happened, and if they're not touched they'll die." She also organized an educational program on nutrition for children's parents at the same hospital.

Darlene feels that helping children get a grip on the world—some sense of their own strengths and abilities in coping and surviving and contributing—is her main goal for children. "I like seeing kids achieve. That's the reward for me. I like being right there when it happens. I like the here and now of intimacy."

Joey was a very fragile child when he started at the center. If he was asked to pick up a piece of paper he would cry and say, "I can't." He was small for his age and had a constant nosebleed. Slowly, patiently Darlene found things that Joey could do, and connected those new things for him to try. In little ways his confidence grew, step by step, and day by day he got a firmer hold on himself. "Now he can even say 'No!' to me," Darlene laughs. "And his nosebleeds have all but disappeared. For me that makes it all worthwhile."

Successes are small and are interspersed with defeats. Valerie was so nervous when she arrived that she shuddered whenever she was touched. After months she began to open up a little, to play in dress-up, to ask questions, and to sit on Darlene's lap. "Valerie's mother was just diagnosed as having cancer," Darlene says.

The turnover of families is also hard emotionally and makes the creation of a coherent program problematic. "Joey is leaving at the end of the month," Darlene says. "It's always hard saying good-bye, but leaving means he'll have a real home, and hopefully his family is going to make it. There's nothing I can do to prepare for this. When they leave here, I'll never see them again. It's not like some neighborhood day care where kids can come to visit or where you see them on the street." She makes a "Good-bye Book" for each child who leaves, and keeps artwork and photos for the others to remember their friend.

"I worry about them in another school," Darlene says. "I'm worried people will look down on them. They need to play dress-up and blocks, and to play with clay and paint, and I worry that their new school will be set-up for computers and reading scores."

Darlene is reminded of James, who had been homeless for all of his five years. He ran a lot and yelled some. He didn't talk, and he never looked an adult in the eye. Over time he learned to play a little and to have an occasional back-and-forth conversation. "He struck me as a normal kid who was environmentally deprived," she says. "Will they see that in kindergarten?"

Darlene shows me a school essay written by the 12-year-old brother of one of her children. It reads in part:

> As I lay in bed crying myself to sleep in the Prince George Hotel, the largest hotel used to house homeless families in New York City, I could not bring myself to overcome the fear of what was happening to me. Over and over again I keep telling myself that I don't deserve this. I'm only 12 years old. I feel so alone. People in school call me a hotel kid. . . . It seems like people are so afraid of ending up where I'm at that they want to punish me for reminding them that being homeless is possible. They have no right to punish me for something I have no control over. I'm just a little boy living in a hotel, petrified, wanting to know what's going to happen to me.

Darlene's center is organized with this brutal context in mind. "Routines are important to these kids. They need strong expectations and definitions in order to get going. I do Circle the same way every day. I give lots of warning and reminders with every transition. They need predictability because their lives are so unpredictable."

There is a lot of space for fantasy and imagination. A favorite game of the dress-up area is playing "Hotel." Eli comes to school in his pajamas and always wants to be the baby, never the brother or the daddy. He needs to be cared for and tucked in his bed by Ebony in his room in the hotel.

"These kids have a hole in their trust," Darlene says. "That hole needs to be repaired. Some of them, on the street, will just go off with anyone. That's not trusting, that's passive and inappropriate. We play a lot of peek-a-boo and hide-and-seek, those kinds of things. We kind of go back to the beginning."

A lot of Darlene's work is basic. She plays and teaches kids who have never played how to do it. She models care, consistency, respect, and the possibility of a better life. "A lot of these kids only know how to make contact through violence," she says. She draws out their hidden lives and shows them new and appropriate ways to make contact with each other and with the world. She nurtures and pushes: "These kids need respect and they need self-respect. They need someone to tell them, 'You can do it, you can make it!' As their teacher I encourage them and I challenge them."

It's mid-afternoon and Darlene, with four children, is walking down the block from the center to a nearby playground. There is a vacant lot cluttered with wrecked automobiles and broken glass. In an alley with a chain-link fence is a battered, broken-down delivery truck, a pile of old tires, and, incongruously, a huge white yacht on cinder blocks with an American flag flapping at the stern. Maurice says, "Don't step on that man," as the little line of walkers snakes past someone passed out on the sidewalk. The street is littered with garbage, and a block away two hookers lean in a doorway smoking. The walkers pass by a group of men playing cards on the sidewalk, using a little box for a table, and everyone calls out friendly greetings. They pass a fried-chicken restaurant and a little bodega, then two deserted buildings whose broken doors and gaping windows stare back at the children. It is a whole landscape of abandonedness.

The playground is under an enormous bridge and is littered with broken fences and scattered glass. There is a lot of traffic noise and no sunlight. Somehow the children see beyond it and fashion the games all children play: tag, chase, and their favorite, hide-and-seek. With this as a background, Darlene continues, "You know, the ones who are always hurt are the powerless ones: children, women, people of color. A few years ago this would have been unimaginable. Now we see it everywhere."

Darlene calls herself a teacher in whatever she does. She imagines learning more about play therapy and women's therapy, taking her teaching into wider areas, but also always with the children. She is a person who calls homelessness unacceptable and offers her own life, energy, and commitment as opposition. Hers is a demanding and transcendant life in teaching.

Darlene called to say that she has been involved in several conferences on homelessness recently. "I spoke about curriculum that builds self-esteem in homeless children, and I talked about Joey and how long and slow it is, but also how rewarding. The key thing is consistency and really caring, creating points of contact with success." Darlene also reported that they built a new playground in the vacant lot next door. "We have a deck, slides, a sandbox, and a garden. It's wonderful. You should come back and see, because what you wrote is too depressing."

# ☆ 7 ☆

# MAYA
# Teaching Heads, Hands, and Hearts

Maya Dawson has been teaching for 34 years, the last 24 of them at the Children's School. She is a widow and has one son and a four-year-old grandchild who is "a delight."

Kindergarten is so firmly established in many communities that it is hardly thought of as preschool, but is instead considered simply the first year of school. In some places, however, kindergarten is still contended, and the recent movement for all-day kindergarten programs in public schools has been hard-fought. All-day kindergartens are seen by some people as responsive to today's families and crucial to today's youngsters, and by many as a sensible extension of the democratic ideal embedded in the establishment of free and common public schools.

However, there is a danger in the assumption that kindergarten is simply the first year of school, and that danger is linked to the taken-for-granted notion of what school itself is. If the common sense of school life includes passivity and conformity, then school has only a tenuous link to learning, because people learn primarily through active engagement with materials, situations, people, and ideas in the world around them. We learn in unique, idiosyncratic, and uneven ways, by exploring, posing questions, experimenting, discovering—just like kindergartners. The danger is that traditional classroom practices with their rows of desks, their textbooks and worksheets, will invade the kindergarten. Instead, we might look forward with hope to the impact that kindergarten—with its experiential, child-centered approach, its commitment to individual children with a wide range of different interests and abilities, its nurturing and yet challenging environment—could begin to have on first and second grades, and then schooling at all levels.

It's 9 AM and fourteen five-year-olds are involved in the serious business of block building. Two are sprawled on the floor, trying to figure out if the tunnel they've made is big enough to accommodate the trucks and cars they're using. Three others are putting the finishing touches on a tower that is considerably taller than they are themselves: One decorates the spaces between the levels with an intricate pattern of color cubes, while the other two alternate small cylinders with triangles spiraling upward, counterclockwise, on the outer edge of each level. They move purposefully back and forth to the block cubbies, getting what they need, over and around houses and bridges and stores that are in various stages of construction. One child has taken down her house and is beginning work on a massive restaurant. Two other children ask if they can help, and when she agrees, they sit down and join the work. A few children have gone to a corner of the room and are cutting out cardboard figures of animals and people to use with the structures they've made or are making signs on construction paper to tape onto their buildings: "The Chinese-Japanese Restaurant," "Tramway—Keep Out," "My house."

Vanessa hunches over the table with her tongue protruding, her hand and whole self curled around the stubby pencil, etching out each letter with great and sustained effort: THE HOLL OF JUSTICE IN OR OUT BY TRAN TRAC OR PICT UP IN SENTRUL BORC.

When she's finished, her shoulders and face relax, she straightens up, smiles, and calls, "Look, Maya!" She waves her sign to the teacher. Maya takes the sign and reads it aloud: "The Hall of Justice. In or out by train track or picked up in Central Park." Maya smiles. "This is wonderful, Vanessa. Put it on your building, and when you're done with it, give this to me."

Vanessa, beaming, says, "Okay," and skips off to the blocks with her sign.

Sarah looks up from her work and asks, "Why do you want that sign, Maya?"

"Oh, teachers have to keep some of your work, some records of what you do."

"Records?" Sarah asks.

"Not phonograph records, not the kind you play on a record player, but notes about what you do and examples of your work."

Back at the table with her coffee and an adult visitor, Maya chuckles. "Sarah's always noticing what I do, always checking up on me. She's going to be either a teacher or a spy."

Does it make children self-conscious when you share with them knowledge of what you do as a teacher?

"Not at all. We're all here together, we're all sharing space and time and activity, we're all involved in a common endeavor. And so we are in that sense a community. But within that community I have a special role. I'm the teacher; I have specific responsibilities and authority. It makes the children secure to know that, it makes them free to feel and to learn. When you see a classroom where the teacher is fuzzy about who she is, you'll see children who are fuzzy about who they are. And that makes it more difficult for them to get their work done."

Maya articulates with precision. Her voice is warm and soft, with a reminder of the rural South only in the slowness and sweetness of her speech. She is trim and energetic, a medium Afro forming a black halo around her open, friendly face. Her hands are in motion as she talks, softly hammering home a point, underlining a word, sweeping away an argument.

"I like to talk and I like to listen," she says. "I think language is a very important part of my life and of our lives. Language is one of the areas I share with children comfortably and easily."

Whether Maya is talking with an adult or a child, her speech, her tone, her language are the same. She doesn't patronize children, and she doesn't talk down to them. There is none of the drawn-up authoritarianism of some teachers in her voice, nor is there the sugar-coated sing-song condescension of others. She speaks directly, and easily, allowing and expecting an honest back-and-forth exchange. She uses the word appropriate to her thought and her feeling, whether it's on any educator's list of words-approved-for-the-preschool-child or not. "Kids delight in language," she says. "They find joy in it as well as understanding, and so do I."

The conversation returns to Vanessa's sign. "Now there's a bright kid. Do you see what she's done? Her strategies for figuring out how to write the words she doesn't know are absolutely brilliant. My favorite is 'Sentrul Borc.' Vanessa has integrated the important qualities it takes to be a good reader. She knows that language has meaning, a very personal meaning to her as well as meaning in a more general sense. She knows that written language is an expression of spoken language, that reading is a process of decoding symbols, and that sounds are related to letters. As her experience with written language becomes broader, she'll see that park is spelled p-a-r-k. It will be her own discovery, and she'll assimilate that knowledge easily and naturally."

There's an old joke among teachers that holds that it's a blessing that educators and politicians haven't yet added speaking to reading, writing, and arithmetic as the "basics" of a standard education. If that should happen, the joke maintains, some social scientist somewhere would develop a curriculum, a lesson plan, and a basic text. Then the spoken word would be reduced to its component parts and given to babies and toddlers a step at a time. They would be expected to master the consonants first, then regular vowels. A long list of one-syllable words would be taught before two-syllable words could be attempted. Songs like "Sing a Song of Sixpence" and "This Train Is Bound for Glory" would be discouraged as potentially confusing and certainly inappropriate. And, of course, the result of all this expense and effort would be a generation that couldn't talk.

Thomas comes to Maya with a problem. "Someone took two of my little blocks." He's frowning, somewhere between sad and angry, and his brow is deeply creased.

"What do you mean, 'Someone took them?'" asks Maya.

"Well, I don't really know. Except when I turned around they were gone from my building."

"They were gone?"

"Yes. I was playing over there, and then when I came back two blocks were missing."

"Okay," says Maya. "See if you can find two more on the shelves and go back to work."

Thomas slumps off in the direction of the block cubbies with his hands deep in his pockets, his brow still wrinkled, a thoughtful frown relieved of some but not all of the emotion.

Ben wanders by the table, and Maya asks him if he's made the purple block he'd wanted earlier.

"No, I don't think I want to now."

Ben is fair with pale gray eyes, which are partially hidden by a shock of white hair falling to his face. His blond eyebrows and lashes wash out his features, and his small frame appears tiny in his big red overalls.

"But you wanted a purple block very much a while ago," Maya says.

"You know, Maya, I know a way it wouldn't work."

Maya smiles. "Yes, I'm sure there are lots of ways it wouldn't work, Ben, but let's concentrate on a way it *would* work."

"But the purple paper is in the art room."

"That's right, but you can go get it."

"Naw."

Sarah is near enough to see and here what is unfolding between Maya and Ben. "I'll go with you, Ben," she says definitively.

Ben lights up and grins at Sarah. "Okay. Good." They run off holding hands.

Maya smiles again. "So that was it. He wanted to make that purple block so much, but he didn't want to go for the paper alone. Good for Sarah."

As Ben is wheeling out the door, Thomas is returning with his problem. His frown has deepened again; he wants Maya to see that this problem is of some importance and that it's not something easily solved. "Maya," he says with a heavy sigh. "There aren't any blocks just like the ones I had."

"No?"

"No." He sits down heavily to punctuate the point.

"Well, is there any block substitute that will work, or anything that you can make?" Maya asks.

"No, Maya. I *need* my blocks back." His voice is rising into a whine, his patience strained.

"Okay, Thomas, I'll try to find the ones you were using." Maya walks to where the children are building and asks them to quiet down. "Please stop what you're doing for a moment. Quiet, please." When the group has quieted sufficiently, she explains the problem. "Thomas, describe the blocks you were using."

"Well, they were small and someone took them."

"But what color were they?" Maya asks. "What shape?"

"Well, they were small triangles, and they were natural color." Thomas's eyes are cast down, and he's shuffling his feet self-consciously.

A few children ask questions—Where had they been? Why don't you use these others instead?—but most return quietly to their work. It's quickly apparent that Thomas's day will have to go forward without the two natural-colored triangles.

"I don't know how to solve this problem," Maya says. "But thank you for trying." And to Thomas she adds, "This time you'll have to find a substitute." Thomas thinks a minute and then says, "Okay." For the first time his voice is light, his face relaxed.

Perhaps all the effort and attention validated his feelings, told him his needs and desires were worthy of respect here, and perhaps that was enough for him. Perhaps that recognition, that affirmation, was the fundamental need, and the blocks were only incidental. And if this is so, imagine what a different experience might have unfolded for Thomas (and for the whole group and for Maya) had his first statement been met with disapproval: "Thomas, you're always complaining." "Well, you'll just have to make do with what's there." "Don't start an argument, Thomas." "Only babies whine." Instead, Maya allowed Thomas to trust himself because she accepted what he felt as valid. She tuned into the world as he saw it instead of insisting that he experience the world as she sees it, judging the weaknesses in his view of things or trying to tell him what he should see or feel. An essential building block to mental health for a child is learning to trust his or her inner reality. Thomas was given that opportunity this day.

Just before time for Meeting, Ben walks over to Maya with his purple block. He's taped a cut-out square of purple paper onto every face of a small cube. "Hey, look!" Ben cries, his arm fully extended, the purple block perched delicately toward the end of his fingers. "Look Maya, a purple block."

"You did it, Ben. I'm glad."

Friday is block day in Maya's class. Blocks are available every day, but on Friday all tables are pushed back, materials are cleared away, and the entire room becomes the block area, the work space for blocks. "This way three or four kids don't dominate the block play," Maya says. "It gives everyone an equal chance, girls as well as boys, and I find that children are moved to try blocks at other times because of our experiences on block day. I want everyone to work with blocks because I think blocks offer more problem-solving opportunities than any other material in the classroom."

There are several kinds of blocks in the classroom—bristle blocks, table blocks, hollow blocks, unfix cubes, cuisinaire rods, dominoes, pattern blocks—but the blocks of block day are the hardwood unit blocks, or Pratt blocks. These blocks consist of shapes, all multiples or divisions of the "basic unit," 1-3/8″ × 2-3/4″ × 5-1/2″. Besides the unit, half unit, double unit, and quadruple unit, there are pillars, small triangles, large triangles, columns, curves, ramps, switches, arches, and more. The unit blocks have a solidity, a weight, and a size that seem to be perfect for the hands of small builders. And their simplicity and logic invite creative construction, intricate patternmaking, and a seemingly endless chain of discoveries. The back wall of Maya's classroom is a row of low cubbies holding hundreds and hundreds of these unit blocks.

Unit blocks were developed by Caroline Pratt, with Harriet Johnson and Lucy Sprague Mitchell, at the City and Country School in New York City in the early 1920s. Through intensive observation over many years, they were able to document the importance of playing with blocks and other concrete materials to the growth, learning, and development of children. Caroline Pratt (1948) wrote in *I Learn From Children*:

> I couldn't have asked for a more appropriate demonstration of my belief in the serious value of children's play. Michael was so deeply absorbed, so purposeful in his construction that he might have been a scientist working out an experiment in a laboratory. The likeness was no accident. He was precisely that, on his own level. He was not merely pushing blocks around; he was not even merely learning what could be done with blocks. With blocks to help him, he was using all his mental powers, reasoning out relationships—the relationship of the delivery wagon to the store, the coal cart loaded from the barge in the river and carrying its load to the home— and he was drawing conclusions. He was learning to think. (p. 32)

These pioneering teachers believed in and demonstrated principles that are widely accepted and practiced in good preschools today, but were heresy 75 years ago: that children are active learners and that they are driven by an internal desire to grow into self-sufficiency and competence. These teachers discovered many of the ways in which play is the serious work of childhood, not something frivolous and wasteful, but a method of understanding and mastering reality. One testament to the early work of Caroline Pratt is the sets of unit blocks to be found in thousands of preschools and kindergartens across the country today.

The nature of any material defines both its limitations and its possibilities. Blocks are hard, solid, regular, angular, and smooth. They are not malleable like clay or Play-Doh, they don't flow or drip like water or paint, they are relatively indestructible. Because blocks are a sensual material, they are soothing and calming for many children. George, whose activity is random and unfocused much of the time, spends an uninterrupted hour of purposeful, concentrated effort with blocks almost every morning. Because they are dependable and predictable, blocks offer a safe, secure field for many children. One can make a tower, a house, a school, a hospital, a road, or a boat, but the block remains the same after all. The very solidity of blocks, their hard, objective definition, allows children to come back to them over several years, investing subjective thoughts and feelings to achieve different, exciting results again and again.

The young child or first-time block builder gets to know the material by touching, holding, and often carrying a block or two around the room on other business. When building begins, children tend to build roads or other horizontal rows of blocks and then to stand blocks one upon another until the increasingly precarious towers crash to the floor. With some experience, children begin to bridge, connecting two blocks with a third, and then to enclose space—two engineering feats necessary to move on to more advanced structures. Soon children are creating delightful patterns with blocks, elaborate fantasies, bold creations that seem held together by gossamer threads. The block builders in Maya's room fall mostly into the class of sophisticated practitioners, for they are building representational structures marked by detail and symbolic reproduction, and they are using their buildings for animated dramatic play.

"Block play is many things to children," says Maya, "but problem solving is at the center of it all." It's true. Thomas and Ben both had problems, and both thought and worked for a long time to solve their problems. Emily and Brendan have a conflict over space; every time Emily stretches out to move a car through her tunnel, she kicks into a section of Brendan's sprawling museum and knocks over a wall or an entire wing. They have to solve a problem about self in space, sharing and mastering space. Angola is making a truck by rolling a double unit with two half units stacked on top of it over two small columns. As she pushes the truck along, the body rolls over the columns and inevitably crashes every couple of feet. After fifteen minutes of rolling, watching, and crashing, Angola goes to the cubbies for two more columns and pushes her truck along slowly over all four columns. This time, as a column emerges at the back of a double unit, Angola grabs it and puts it in front of the oncoming truck. The truck rolls along without crashing, Angola busily pushing the double unit with one hand and keeping the columns moving from rear to front with the other. A slight smile emerges, yet her sparkling eyes remain fixed on her work. Angola has solved her problem and invented a moving truck with blocks.

Block play provides children with other opportunities for learning. They learn with their hands that two unit blocks are the same as a double unit, long before they encounter the abstract "one plus one equals two."

And although they cannot explain it yet, they know in a deep, bodily way the truths of mathematics because they have discovered them themselves. They have already seen a thousand examples of more than, the same as, less than, about the same as, and so on. They already know about shape, space, harmony, relationship, balance, equilibrium, gravity, three-dimensionality, angles, and a host of related concepts because they need these things in order to play. At the same time their language is pushed and extended as they speak about what their hands are doing: above, below, beside, thick, thin. Math is a way to describe the physical world, and the block builders are already mathematicians and scientists and problem solvers because of their sophisticated experiential base. Their hands and then their minds understand what Thomas means when he says, "two natural-colored triangles."

On block day, the morning Meeting in Maya's class is given over entirely to talk about buildings. "Okay," says Maya when everyone has gathered, sitting on knees or bottoms facing her. "Let's talk about your buildings. Noah, why don't you and Ben start."

Noah begins an enthusiastic monologue practically before Maya finishes her sentence. "My building is a restaurant and it's called the Chinese-Japanese Restaurant," he says, looking intently at the pile of blocks near the middle of the room. He pops up off his knees and hurries to the building, where he drops down again and continues gesturing with both hands. "When the cook makes the food, it's outside the building over here, and so the waiters and waitresses have to carry food in bags so it doesn't get cold. Over here there's tables and chairs for the customers." He goes on describing the detail of his work with precision: waiters and waitresses, outside the building, customers, and cooks. When he's finished, he relaxes into a satisfied slump, smiling to himself. Maya says, "It looks like a very good restaurant, Noah. Ben, why don't you tell us more about the restaurant?"

"Well, I don't really want to talk about it," says Ben shyly.

"Would you like to talk about something else?" asks Maya.

"Well, yes," says Ben, his voice gaining strength. "I really want to talk about how I made this." He holds up the purple block and turns it triumphantly.

"Okay, that's a fine idea," says Maya, her eyes smiling. There's a sweet, low laugh in her voice again, but it neither mocks nor belittles. Rather it is the sound of self-satisfaction, the sound of a productive teacher. "Why don't you describe exactly how you made it? Tell us what you did first and what you did after that."

Ben warms up and starts enthusiastically, looking only at the block as he speaks, turning it occasionally, examining it, then holding it out for others to see. "Well, first I cut off a piece of purple paper. Then I let it rest on the table while I got some tape and put it here. Then, see it used to be a plain block, a natural-colored block. Then I put this here and then I did it over and over and over."

When he's finished, Maya says, "Give it to me for a minute, Ben." He hands it over and Maya holds it up. "You can see over here how he made it," she says, peeling back one edge where there's no tape. "And it's quite a good job. Ben wanted a purple block and so he had to figure out how to do it. What's important to understand is that sometimes when there's something you want, you have to figure out how to get it."

"You have to use your brain," Thomas adds knowingly.

"Right," says Maya. "You have to use your brain and your hands, and you have to work. Ben said it took a long time, and he kept working until he got it finished." Maya hands the block to Ben.

"It took a long time," Ben agrees. "And I don't want to take the paper off."

"Well," Maya chuckles to herself. "We'll take it off at clean-up time because that's a pretty important rule about blocks—when we use tape on them, we have to take it off."

"But not soon," Ben says hopefully.

"Well, not right now," agrees Maya.

"Like maybe tomorrow," says Ben.

"No, it'll be today, but, Ben, you can take it off yourself."

Ben pauses thoughtfully. "Can I keep the paper?" he asks.

"Yes, that's a good idea. Put the paper in your cubby."

Here is that sense of mutual respect once more. Maya takes Ben's feelings seriously because she recognizes that he takes them seriously and that taking one's feelings seriously is an important part of growing up whole and healthy. She allows him his emotional life, trying neither to control it nor to manipulate it. She finds a way to empathize with Ben, to respond to his needs without being defined or debilitated by them. This, too, is important: She thinks enough of the rule and routine of the group that she doesn't change it easily. But neither does she sacrifice Ben's feelings. Ben comes through affirmed and confident.

After several more children describe their buildings and after a few more animated exchanges, it's time to clean up. Maya again shares a sense of herself as a special person, a teaching person, a decision maker and a leader in the classroom. "Today I didn't put out the paper so soon, and I'm glad because I think you finished your buildings and played for a longer time." She is allowing access to her thinking as a teacher, which also allows the children to reflect about their own roles, responsibilities, and activity. There's general agreement that this has been a particularly productive block day, with only one dissent. "I wanted more time to make my purple block," says Ben. Maya smiles her agreement.

Cleaning up the blocks is a flurry of activity, a blurring of work/play characteristic of the preschool classroom. No one seems to see clean-up as drudgery; rather, each child approaches it as an extension of the work of building. "If you have any signs or cardboard people that you're going to save, go and get them now." Maya begins. "Ben, you can work on your purple block." Ben and four other children rush into the sprawling block-scape to retrieve precious creations. "Okay," she continues. "Now I need two people for a serious job at the table." Hands fly up, and Maya selects two children. "Be sure the glue has a top on it and the scissors are back on the rack." Maya continues assigning jobs, two children to pick up all the round shapes, one for colored cubes, two to work only on quadruple units. Everyone is busy. Nothing is knocked down or thrown into a pile. Buildings are unbuilt, block by block, and stacked according to size and shape. Then cubbies begin to fill up, unit blocks in one, double units in another, triangles over here, columns over there.

After about 10 minutes, Maya asks everyone to stop. "Let's rest a moment and see where we are," she says. Everyone stops. Maya suggests a few deep breathing exercises, which make Vanessa and Sarah giggle. "Okay," she says. "I think we're more than halfway done. Let's have another three children work on this section here." Again hands shoot up and work begins. Some children hurry back and forth to the cubbies; others are more interested in the taking down and stacking. Angola and Noah make little trains of blocks and push them across the room to put them away. Everyone participates, each in his or her own way. In about 15 minutes everything is in place and order has returned. It's time to go outside, and there's a scramble of coats and hats and mittens.

The Children's School has existed in New York City for the past fifty years—a three-story red brick box rising out of the concrete, surrounded by half a dozen Greenwich Village trees, forlorn yet courageous things, anchored in the cement much as the vandal-proof benches with which they share the sidewalk. On this February morning, as a bitter wind drives a cold drizzle down the Hudson River and through the bones of the city hiker, the name of the school announces itself on the west side of the building in faded yellow letters visible a block away. A little further down on the same wall a cracked whitewashed board is fixed to the brick, and "The Children's School" is written out in gay red script.

Inside, the visitor is greeted by the warm voice and golden smile of the receptionist. Children move easily from the downstairs cafeteria to the science room and the computer center, from the gym back to class upstairs or down to the wood shop.

On the wall of a first-floor office is a blown-up photograph of the founder of the Children's School, along with these words:

> The school will not always be just what it is now, but we hope it will be a place where ideas can grow, where heresy will be looked upon as possible truth, and where prejudice will dwindle from lack of room to grow. We hope it will be a place where freedom will lead to judgment—where ideals year after year are outgrown like last season's coat for larger ones to take their places.

Up one flight of stairs to the left is the five-year-olds' classroom. Maya and her assistant Barry sit at a small table near the entrance, greeting children and parents as they arrive and discussing plans for the day. The early arrivals are busy in the room, which is organized into activity areas: an ample, obvious block area, a cozy, inviting book corner, a dress-up space, child-sized tables and chairs near the art materials and manipulatives. A large bathroom across from the entrance contains two toilets just the right size for five-year-olds, two low, deep-tub sinks, and lots of extra room for storage. A large, squat teacher's desk and chair sit against one wall, with a sign identifying the area as the "Doctor's Office." A poster taped to the desk shows "What a Healthy Newborn Baby Looks Like." The poster is one of those distributed by the Public Health Service, simple but complete, technical but accessible. On a table behind the desk are books about the human body—*My Five Senses, Look at Your Eyes, This Can Lick a Lollipop, Bodies*—and books about birth—*We are Having a Baby, Gabriell's First Birthday, All Kinds of Babies*. The collection includes books and pictures of black and other Third World children as well as white ones. And there is a range of choices from simple picture stories to more sophisticated books.

"We just found out that Ben's mother is having a baby," Maya explains. "And so we set this up last week. Ben's enjoying this immensely." Much of Maya's curriculum begins with the children themselves—their specific needs, interests, and life experiences. Maya believes that young children learn best when they are in a warm and loving environment, when they are allowed to experience life whole and integrated, and when they can follow their own powerful desires to learn and to grow.

Teachers look for ways to deepen and extend knowledge, to connect the known to the unknown, to find what is salient for each particular child, to discover how to develop, expand, and feed over time. Teachers try to provide opportunities for experiences that build on previous experiences and that at the same time lay the foundation for new experiences. In Maya's class a curriculum unit on birth is unfolding now because a mother is pregnant.

On one wall is an engaging poster of penguins standing in a row, which is repeated four times, giving the impression of hundreds of penguins standing in a long winding line for a bank machine or a supermarket checkout, talking, telling stories, arguing. They look almost human. "They do look human," agrees Maya. "And kind of soft and cuddly. But you know, they're really pretty tough, vicious with strong beak-like jaws. And they fight a lot."

Penguins are a big part of Maya's classroom this year. One bookshelf is given over entirely to penguin books: *A Penguin Year, Antarctica, Mr. Popper's Penguins, Penguins, Of All People.* One book is called *The Baby Penguin,* a homemade book with children's drawings on each page. It's made of cardboard, covered with clear contact paper, bound with metal loops, and says:

> The baby penguin is inside the egg. I know that. The baby penguin breaks its way out of the egg. I know that. The egg tooth is on her bill. I know that. The baby penguin hatches soaking wet from having been immersed in fluids while in the egg. I know that. After the baby dries he has a warm fluffy coat of down feather. I know that. The baby penguins have voracious appetites. I know that. The baby penguins go to sea when they are about nine weeks old. I know that.

There are those big words again—voracious, immersed, fluids. And yet, to listen to five- or even three-year-olds with a large language base in their lives makes it obvious that language is an acquired skill. Children don't know which words are hard and which are easy. If they are encouraged to express their thoughts and their feelings, if they are in an environment where words are freely used, their language grows and develops and the words come out.

Three striking children's paintings are framed and decorate one wall. The first is a black-and-white work entitled "Millions and Millions of Penguins." Next to it is a brightly colored impressionistic work, with lots of thick paint and the clear black outline of a penguin head in profile smack in the middle, called "This Penguin Is Marching to the Rookery." Finally there is a painting of a stuffed shirt in motion on an orange background with a written comment: "There are many kinds of penguins. The Adelie penguins and the emperor penguins live in the cold, cold, cold Antarctica."

"I was intrigued with the life-style of penguins," Maya says. "I remember discovering that the father penguin is very involved with taking care of the egg, and thinking, 'This is delightful!' And I was interested in the South Pole, which I find fascinating. So this is a little teacher stimulus, something I can discover with the children and stay interested and involved in myself."

Angola and two other children are sitting at the table looking at the latest issue of *Ranger Rick*, a popular children's magazine published by the National Wildlife Federation. The February issue, which has just arrived, is coincidentally a "Special Issue on Antarctica," with a cover photograph of a penguin standing on an ice floe. "Isn't the whole world studying penguins?" Maya asks in mock surprise. "I see them everywhere, and it can't be a coincidence." She laughs and adds, "Young children are egocentric, you know, and I've lived with them for a long time. I guess I'm that way, too."

Angola is showing *Ranger Rick* to her friends and talking about penguins. "See, these are Adelie penguins," she says, pronouncing the word correctly, uh-*day*-lee. Her large, dark eyes are focused on the picture, her expressive face showing concentration, surprise, confusion, and delight as she turns the pages. Her dark hair is tied in two tight braids, and she is wearing a bright pink dress. "And this is the rookery. See this? I don't know what it is." She pauses, and someone says that it's a leopard seal trying to eat a penguin. "Well, it looks disgusting," Angola says definitively.

"I wanted to see if I could sustain a study with fives over a full year," says Maya. "Keeping up the interest and excitement. I wanted to see if we could hold on to it. I believe that teachers have to help children develop passion. And, of course, you have to express your interest and excitement. So I look for something—anything—around which to get passionate. A little bit of this and a little bit of that isn't the best way for me. Let's get into a study thoroughly, fully, for all it's worth! Let's chew on it and turn it around! And out of it let's plan activities in reading, math, science, and social studies. Let's have the interest in penguins teach us whatever we need to know." She pauses for a moment.

"Well, I'm delighted to report that these children are more excited about penguins now than they were six months ago. And they're consistent. Not a day goes by that someone doesn't bring in a picture of a penguin or information they've found to share with the class. It's a sustained study, and I'm convinced that these five-year-olds will carry some of that knowledge and appreciation for penguins their whole lives. And whatever they do next, they'll carry a good feeling to it because they did this study in depth."

Without penguins Maya's classroom would still be a good preschool classroom. The children would, of course, bring their concerns, their fantasies, their investigations, and their investments. It has all the materials, ideas, and basic elements upon which to build. But Maya thinks that the penguins bring a richness and a depth of feeling that is missing in some classes. For Maya, the penguins offer concrete material with which to work on the cognitive skills and a lot of the affective skills as well. Penguins provide a field for investigation and discovery; they make learning and growth visible and persuasive with this preschool group.

A child runs up to Maya and throws himself into her lap. His eyes are wet and his voice is tight, strained. "He's running over me," he cries. Maya hugs him but remains seated, barely moving, unruffled.

"What do you mean, 'he's running over you?'" Maya asks gently.

"He's stepping on my blocks," he blurts out, his face flushed with tension.

A second child shuffles over, his hands stuffed deep into his pockets, with the unmistakable look of five-year-old guilt on his face. "Well, it was in the wrong place and it was an accident, Maya." His eyes wander everywhere except to Maya's face and his voice is thin, pleading.

Maya reassures the first child. "Go on back to your work. It was an accident and he's sorry." To the second child she says softly, "All right, go back to the blocks, Brendan. You had that same accident yesterday, so be careful." Brendan hurries off.

"You have to accept that conflict among children is not always negative," Maya says. "It can offer tremendous opportunities for learning, for working things out, for finding alternatives. Children learn an awful lot through conflict. I think kids work harder on alternatives to conflict because problems arise in natural situations and the stakes become very important to them. You can't teach social skills, conflict resolution, and respect for others from a book. You have to live it. And if you're a child, you sometimes need someone there to guide you through it."

Accepting conflict as a natural part of the preschool classroom frees the teacher to search for ways to resolve situations without feeling she has failed. The teacher is further relieved of focusing on right and wrong, punishment and blame, and becomes interested in solutions. "I talk with children about conflict, not always at the moment, but often in the morning Meeting," Maya says. "When conflict occurs, we already have a base of understanding, a frame of reference. I want to help them to learn those processes of how to go about solving problems, working them out, how you go about living together and getting the things you need and want."

Maya brings empathy for children to her understanding of discipline. She sees the world through their eyes and tries to respond to their needs. When she becomes angry, she expresses her anger, but she doesn't attack, shame, ridicule, threaten, or insult. She wants the children to come through conflict and disagreement strengthened, not wounded. Maya models good discipline by showing the children self-discipline, good manners, compassion, and respect.

Maya gets up and walks to the tables where several children are cutting paper and creating collages. "Guys," she says. "Guys, can you quiet down a little?"

A voice says, "Oh, no. You're going to say, 'Five more minutes.' "

Maya laughs and says, "Yes, I am. And I want you to start to get ready."

The same voice complains, "Oh, no! Clean-up."

"Not yet," says Maya. "But soon. And I want you to pick up these scraps of paper on the floor."

Soon there is a tornado of clean-up activity. In no time the room is neat and tidy, and kids are pushing and dragging chairs into a large circle for their morning Meeting. "The Meeting is part of our routine," says Maya. "And it's very important. It's a time to exchange information, to share ideas, reflect, and think. Routine is important to children because it gives them a sense of security. They know we are consistent, that there are things they can count on. I like to keep patterns going so the children can depend on them. When there's going to be a change, I give plenty of advance notice so they can prepare." Routine is part of the structure of the classroom, and structure includes the materials, schedule, room arrangements, and people the children can expect to be more or less consistent throughout the year. An open preschool classroom like Maya's has a definite structure and routine, even though it is not easily apparent to a casual onlooker. An appropriate structure and routine liberate children to think and feel more broadly and more easily than if there were no dependable base or anchor.

"Be very quiet," Maya says softly. "Very quiet. Shhh. Let's have a quiet moment." Maya's own calm begins to spread and settle deeply into the room. The mood is practically meditative. "Good. Now we have a busy day, so let's get to work," Maya says quietly. "Angola's mom brought a tape recorder, and we're going to make a tape for Spring."

A voice cries out sharply, "Hey! Don't push!"

"I don't want to hear about it now, Josh," Maya says firmly. "I really don't. Just solve that without disrupting the group."

"After we make the tape," Maya continues, "Spring and a couple of other kids can go to that little bakery around the corner with Barry and get a cake for our Good-bye Party."

"Oooh!" An eager collective swoon of joy and anticipation sweeps the group, followed by an outburst of individual expression: "I want chocolate!" "I love cake!" "Me too!" "Oh, I love it!"

"Okay," Maya says, "We'll get a cake. If Spring comes early enough we'll have it for snack, and if she comes later we'll have it after lunch."

"I hope she comes early," someone shouts. "Me too! Me too!" And then the long swoon again: "Ooooh!"

"Now, you have to think about what you want to say into the tape recorder," Maya says. "Remember, Spring's going to take the tape with her when her family moves to Italy. And we want her to have a wonderful tape of us to play when she's thinking of New York and school and you."

"I'm going to say, 'Hello, Spring!' " cries Ben.

"And 'I like you,' " says Brendan.

"Make sure you say your name or she won't know who said it," Angola adds wisely.

"That's right, Angola," says Maya. "Everyone say your name. You might also say something about school and remind her of things here or things you did together. Say more than, 'Hello, Spring,' because sometimes when children talk, especially into a tape recorder or on a stage, they repeat the same thing over and over. But that won't make a very interesting tape for Spring. So say more than, 'Hello Spring.' And be very quiet when it's not your turn to talk. Okay, who wants to start?"

Maya calls on Noah to start, and Angola's mother holds the mike near his face while he speaks. "Hello, Spring. I miss you already and I know you'll miss me." Noah's face is flushed, his head is tilted awkwardly, and he's twirling his hair in tight circles with his left thumb and forefinger.

"Say your name," Angola's mother whispers.

"It's Noah," he shouts.

As Angola's mother moves around the circle with the microphone, each child speaks in turn. The group watches, eagerly listening to each, responding with feeling to the sweetness, the humor, the sadness of the moment.

"I miss you as much as I miss ice cream. With the love of Thomas," is followed by an explosion of laughter and great rocking back and forth in chairs.

"Hi, Spring," says Ben in a sweet conversational tone. "I miss you as much as I miss the tree we saw in Battery Park because I haven't seen it in a long time. With all my love." Vanessa smiles as Ben speaks.

"I miss you and I want the chocolate cake," cries Brendan, and again the room rocks with joy.

Maya holds the microphone for a minute, smiling, and then speaks with feeling, "Remember all the fun we had studying about penguins. Remember how they lived in the Antarctic where it's cold, cold, cold. I'll remember all those things and I'll miss you." She pauses and then adds brightly, "It's Maya."

"Spring, I'll miss you," says Angola quietly. "And I hope you have a good time living in Italy."

When every child has spoken, Maya asks if they want to hear it, and they do. As it plays, everyone listens with approval and satisfaction. There is hilarity revisited, sweetness felt again, and embarrassment because no one can fully bear to hear that strange voice that is your own played back electronically.

"That's a lovely tape," says Maya finally. "And I think Spring will like having it in Italy." Spring has still not arrived, so Maya moves on.

"Listen to the plans now," she says. "Yesterday you painted some wonderful penguins. And the day before we painted a beautiful Antarctic background. Today I want some of you to cut out penguins and paste them on the background in the hall."

"Me!"

"Me!"

"Me!"

Maya holds up her hand. "Wait a minute. Quiet now. We'll talk first and then we'll decide who will do what. So some of you will make a mural of millions and millions of penguins. Now, who didn't make a card for Spring?"

"I did!"

"I made a red one."

"No," Maya smiles. "No, my question is who did *not* make a card?"

Not a hand goes up. "Good. Everyone made one."

"I did."

"Yes!"

"Yes."

"Okay, good. Now, I wrote a message on the chalkboard, and I'd like someone to read it." About a half dozen hands shoot up, and these children go the board one at a time to read out loud: "Dear Spring. We Will Miss You."

Maya selects five volunteers to cut out penguins.

"There's a lot of work to do there so you better get right to it. And don't forget to get scissors and paste." Off they go.

"We haven't done little books in a long time. Who wants to do little books at the table?" Ben, Vanessa, and Angola raise their hands and troop off to get supplies. "I'll be over in a minute," Maya calls after them.

"Who wants to play at the water table? Okay, Thomas and Aisha. And remember, one definite rule about the water table is you have to keep the water in the water table," she says with emphasis. "Now, you three can start working with blocks. I'll be there to see how you're doing in a short while."

The room begins to hum, and Maya moves around checking on each little group. She smiles at the block builders as they transform themselves quickly into doctors in a hospital emergency room. "I had a very strong fantasy life when I was a kid," Maya says. "In high school when I was bored I could sit in class and imagine myself all over the world, doing this and doing that, and this quality in children intrigues me. Children fantasize. I feel a lot of closeness to their free style of living, to their honesty, and to their fantasy lives."

"Maya, this eraser doesn't work."

"I'm not going to get involved in that," says Maya. "I'd just as soon you ignored mistakes."

Ben's little book is called *The Penguins*. "I know 'the,'" says Ben, "but I can't spell 'penguin.' I'll go to the dictionary."

"That's a good idea," says Maya. "Where else could you find it?"

"A book," says Vanessa.

"But I think I'll look in the dictionary," says Ben flatly. As he turns the pages of a large children's dictionary, he says to Vanessa, "You should call your book *A Quality Book*."

"But I don't know what 'quality' means," Vanessa objects.

"Well," Ben says, searching for an explanation. "This is a quality crayon and this is a quality pencil. See this shirt?" he asks, pulling his own sleeve. "This is a quality shirt."

Ben finds a picture of a penguin in the "P" section of the dictionary and carefully copies the word into his book.

"To me the world of reading and books is vitally important. It's exciting and joyful," says Maya later. "I tell each child that this year or next year you'll be reading on your own. That's my expectation. I say that reading will be a wonderful part of your life and that you *will* learn."

Books are an important part of the room arrangement. Besides the general story books, in the reading area, books about babies and the human body are grouped in the "Doctor's Office." There is a table of books about penguins, and another table with books about Italy. "All these different books tell us that we can find out all kinds of information from books. The picture books show us that the beauty of the world is there for us. The books on Italy make something strange and distant become close and familiar.

"I put books all over the room so that the children can see that books can be a part of everything else, that they can deepen everything we do, and also so that the children can think about why things are where they are."

There are a number of homemade books in the room—penguin books, storybooks, and a table of books by Maya. "When I was introducing my books, I said, 'I'm going to give you a clue about the author of these books. See if you can figure out who wrote them. It's a woman and a teacher and a black person!' They all shouted, 'You did!'"

All this effort makes books accessible. Anyone can write books, and many, many people do. Producing a book takes work and effort, but it's not a mystery. It gives children critical skills and some power to see that authors have a point of view, an idea, an approach.

"Children need to experience lots of different books," says Maya. "They need to have good literature. They need to have books that mirror for them culturally and socially. They need to have books that expand their world and books that give them information."

Maya is teaching reading by communicating a high expectation to these kids in a low-keyed, nonpressured way. She is teaching reading by creating an environment where books are linked to important emotional and intellectual concerns of the children, where reading is part of loving and learning. She is teaching reading by validating individual experiences and finding ways for each child to succeed in expressing his or her thoughts and feelings. She is affirming in practice that words have importance and power, that reading is not merely a skill or set of rules, but is a link to that power and that ability to realize yourself and to know and be competent in the world.

"You know," Maya says at the end of the day. "From the time I was a little girl I always knew I'd be a teacher. I played teacher with my dolls. I played school with my marbles, setting up different colored marbles for different classes on the rug at home. By the time I was 11 or 12, I was always finding somebody's baby to take care of. So there was always that affinity with young children."

She continues, "I went to school in Savannah, Georgia, and I remember it as a warm, wonderful experience. Mainly I remember friends, crayons, and fun." Maya's grandmother often told her to involve herself in "interesting things," to spend time with interesting people, and especially never to allow anyone to treat her disrespectfully. Maya grew up with a strong sense of being a valuable person and pursuing interesting projects.

Maya went to Howard University, New York University, and Bank Street College of Education. She set up a preschool for blind children at the New York Guild for the Blind, a project that tapped all of her creative resources and inner strengths. Her work at the Children's School for 24 years has been guided by a strong sense of joy in achievement and an abiding respect for all people.

"When I started teaching, I didn't imagine myself teaching for the rest of my life," Maya says. "I saw myself becoming a principal or a director or a teacher in college. But as I went along I realized that I was doing well teaching, that I enjoyed it, that children related to me, and that positive experiences took place in the classroom. So it became important to me to do the work I do best. I couldn't get this much fulfillment from being an administrator, and I also want a certain amount of joy in my life. This world is too tough for a person to work without joy."

She continues, "I feel productive in teaching. I can see my work has results. It's stimulating because I have to keep thinking and creating. I have to keep my mind active. I'm in good physical shape working with little children. It's a healthy way of life. And except for the terrible salary, I feel lucky that I found a career that's so right for me." Teaching for Maya is a "continuous circle," a seamless web. "It's a life," she says, "and there is no line between the person and the teacher."

The paint containers are rinsed and put away. The cubbies are tidied up, and the room is ready for tomorrow. "Each group of children brings new and exciting challenges. Here's all these new personalities. What will they be like? What will we discover? How will we grow as people and as a group? I find that exciting. I don't feel that the work is repetitive because I don't do anything exactly the same. Each day is different. The year starts, and it's a whole new beginning. Here I go again."

Maya plans to stay right where she is—teaching five-year-olds and teaching other teachers. "I try to come from the classroom with the children to the classroom with the adults," she writes. "I try to keep flowing, the same energy, enthusiasm, clarity, honesty, expectations, and humor. Working this way I try to develop a better understanding of the educational process and its political implications. I have learned so much."

# ★ 8 ★

# THE DISCERNING "I"
## Teacher Self-Discovery and Self-Construction Through Autobiography

The promise of an autobiographical method for teachers lies in its ability to expand the available natural history of teaching as well as in its practical, action-oriented stance. Autobiography is a process of self-formation and self-declaration; it is a process that pushes back memory, revealing not only entanglements but also choices. In this way autobiography shows us not only what we've been made, but what we've made of what we've been made (Pinar, 1986). It is a method that connects the inner self to the public self. Autobiography widens the scope of choice and in the process enlarges, hopefully, both the autobiographer and the reader. With respect to the former, a description of the impact of this work on the six teacher-autobiographers is contained in Appendix B.

Of course, writing about a life smoothes it out. There is falseness in the writing. But writing about a life also makes it public, and there is validity in making a public record. This is the tension of autobiography: authenticity versus distortion.

An interpretive stance is essential to make sense of the public, written record. Interpretation here will be an attempt to link these teacher portraits to one another and also to what we know about the cultural and institutional context of teaching. The search for continuities and harmonies will focus on the portraits themselves, but will also look beyond the portraits for linkages with what we know of the larger social realities of teaching. There is a need to uncover those themes that appear to be unique and those that are neither independent nor special. In the search for insight and understanding, there is a need to look at the portraits through the lens of other critics.

### PATTERNS EMERGING FROM THE PORTRAITS

How do the co-biographies, or life-narratives, penetrate the practice of teaching, and how does teaching enter the lives described here? What are the connections, the internal consistencies, and the incongruities? What are the patterns between reflective practitioner, autobiographer, and whole person, and how do these patterns link up across the portraits? What are the continuities and harmonies?

Anna defines her work in the infant-toddler room as creating a home-like environment for children. She thinks of herself as being a substitute mother for a few hours every day, and she struggles to achieve an intensity and investment in each child that will truly support and nurture and challenge. Anna vividly remembers certain things from her own childhood: her parents separating and her being sent to Cuba, feeling humiliated by a teacher who didn't like her, and the pain of separation from loved ones. Her work reminds her of how it feels to be a baby—moods more than details—and puts her in touch with her own childlikeness. This memory, this empathetic joy and pain, Anna claims, makes her better at what she does.

Chana's work with children also vibrates with the issue of separation. She is dealing with toddlers leaving their mothers for the first time, and each day is a drama of drop-offs and pick-ups, rendings and reconciliations. A lot of Chana's energy every day is invested in comforting children and understanding anew and in painful detail the issue of separation for children, for parents, and for herself. Her home is stocked with items she believes will help children cope with and understand separation from their mothers: books, toy telephones, photographs, and tapes from home.

Separation is something about which Chana has thought seriously and come to certain solid conclusions. It is also an issue that resonates deeply in the telling of her own life story. There is a sense in which her own childhood, as the oldest child in a large and loving extended family, provided her with a safe harbor from which to move away. That experience is a strong positive memory for her, and she contrasts her own early life with the stress of the lives of the children she cares for today. Chana thinks of herself as a person who understands what makes separations successful experiences from which to grow and build. She does not believe in glossing over the pain or sadness—she cites the difficult loss of her very special grandfather, for example—but she thinks that the pain can be endured in a context of support and care, and can lead to an enriching and strengthening of life.

JoAnne's favorite times in teaching include moments when she feels she has helped empower a child, moments like teaching a child to put on her own coat or fasten his own overalls, moments like allowing a child to answer the center's phone and take a message. She structures opportunities for children to make decisions. JoAnne is proud of the fact that she raised the money to build a child-sized, empowering bathroom in the center. And the things that JoAnne wants for children are a taxonomy of empowerment: a sense of safety, happiness, confidence, fairness, self-respect, importance. When she thinks of having a daughter, JoAnne imagines inviting her into a world where all the options are open and where she can accomplish anything. In her own teaching, JoAnne values the ways she is direct and honest and nonpatronizing with children, and the ways she develops their sense of self-worth by valuing them, their ideas, and their experiences in a genuine way.

The theme of empowerment is important in JoAnne's autobiographical recollection, too, but primarily in a negative way. She sees that in her life she has always thrived on responsibility, that she loved being asked to do chores in school, for example, or to take on added weight at work, and that she responded by being stronger and more able. But she remembers with pain that her mother gave her few opportunities to feel good about herself and instead communicated a deep and abiding distrust of her. She was never given the meaningful responsibility she wanted; instead she was ignored or treated with contempt. In a sense part of JoAnne's enthusiasm about her work is, she thinks, linked to making her feel responsible and powerful in the world today, even as she helps create for children a central core of power and open possibilities that she was denied as a child.

For Darlene, teaching is part of a life of care and concern for other people. Teaching is a deep passion whose reward is witnessing growth and development in others. Darlene brings that same passion to her family, to the study of the Bible, to her volunteer work with boarder babies, and to her friendships. Darlene's teaching is patient, and it takes time to unfold for each child.

Michele's classroom contains echoes of her own childhood: a nurturing environment for plants, animals, and children that she remembers so clearly, a time to write one's words, which she recalls as engaging and meaningful. At the center of Michele's teaching is a strong valuing of education. She has defined routines, a clearly articulated plan for her room arrangement, and solid traditional goals for children. When she reflects on her teaching, she emphasizes the importance of order and organization and productive work for children.

Michele's life-narrative also suggests this theme strongly. Education was of supreme value to her family. Education was the road to dignity and worth—liberation. Books, for example, were important in her life, and they are important in her classroom. Furthermore, Michele's fifth-grade teacher had a tremendous impact on her as a child. This teacher was educated herself and was an educator, and Michele could see concretely the valuing and value of her life. Teaching was a way to have and live education, to be respected and important to others.

Maya's classroom is an abundantly rich and varied place, where almost any child can find something to engage with and learn from. There are paints and blocks and books and projects and all kinds of weird and wonderful materials. It is an interesting place to be if you are five, because there are interesting things to do and to be, and also because Maya is there to make sure that you engage yourself in interesting work, to be certain that everyone is being fair, and finally to respect you and the choices you make in regard to your own growth and learning.

Maya's strongest memories from childhood have to do with a sense of warmth and respect. When she describes her own family life, one can almost smell the bread baking in the oven and the supper cooking on the stove. She tells stories of her grandmother, who told her to respect herself and never to put herself in situations where she wasn't respected, and who insisted that she associate only with other children who were doing "interesting things." Maya feels a strength to this day from being nurtured and raised in a wide circle of human love and care, something one sees re-created at the Children's School.

There are other continuities and harmonies within and between these portraits. Each of these teachers is deeply engaged in self-criticism and self-reflection. For Michele, there is a sense of wanting to "perfect" her classroom and her work; for Darlene, a desire to return to school and expand her practice; for JoAnne, an "excitement" about thinking about her work and striving to improve it. For Chana, there is a "jarring" that accompanies looking at her work; for Anna, a need to step back soon and take stock of herself; for Maya, an ongoing engagement in planning, organizing, and defining her teaching. For each, there is a sense of growth and change and self-appraisal. The drama is the struggle to teach, to do it better, to get it right. This may, of course, be a result of the writing or telling itself. Those who choose to write and tell their stories are practically by definition those who tend to be self-reflective. Inviting someone to create a life-narrative is also an invitation to reflect and examine.

In these portraits we also see some sense of struggle against officialdom and a defining of oneself in opposition. For Chana, the struggle is direct and consuming; for Darlene, it is urgent and apparent; for JoAnne, it moderates between intense conflict (with the Health Department or the lack of needed money) and absolute calm; and for Michele, it tends to be a background reality that merely threatens to impose. But for each there is a sense of her teaching identity tied up with a struggle against large, impersonal, and ultimately destructive forces. This theme is echoed in the narratives of other teachers, in which they fight to remake the official curriculum, to transcend the prescribed teacher's role, and to resist the imposition of the system in an attempt to teach.

Many well-known teacher-autobiographies (see, for example, Sylvia

Ashton-Warner, 1958, 1963; Herb Kohl, 1967) reveal an abiding struggle to find an authentic teaching voice, a genuine voice that integrates the teaching role with the deepest sense of self, a voice that can link up in dialogue with the voices of others. For Anna, Chana, Darlene, Maya, JoAnne, and Michele, there is also the search for an authentic teaching voice that integrates teaching with the deepest sense of self; that voice is similarly based on dialogue. For Chana, Anna, Darlene, and Michele, teaching is linked to a powerful sense of family values, and for JoAnne and Maya, it is a way of empowering others as well as being powerful in the world oneself. For each, there is a sense of respecting children as they are, and a belief in dialogue with preschoolers, even toddlers and infants, as the most legitimate way to teach.

For these six women, teaching involves a search for meaning in the world. Teaching has become for each a life project, a calling, a vocation that is an organizing center of all other activities. Teaching is past and future as well as present, it is background as well as foreground, it is depth as well as surface. Teaching is pain and humor, joy and anger, dreariness and epiphany. For these six, teaching is world building, it is architecture and design, it is purpose and moral enterprise. Teaching is a way of being in the world that breaks through the boundaries of the traditional job and in the process redefines all life and teaching itself.

"Teaching as identity" is the clearest theme to emerge in this inquiry, and "teaching as identity" is the frame through which each portrait makes sense. In these portraits, there is no clear line delineating the person and the teacher. Rather, there is a seamless web between teaching and being, between teacher and person. Teaching is not simply what one does, it is who one is. Teaching is a life, a way of being in the world, an intentional circle for these six outstanding teachers.

In contrast to the dominant pattern of our society, which defines "personality, achievement, and the purpose of human life in ways that leave the individual suspended in glorious, but terrifying, isolation" (Bellah et al., 1985, p. 6), we see here people whose work is "morally inseparable" (p. 66) from their lives, and whose social commitments are coherent with their private pursuits. These teachers seem to have found ways to speak of values in an environment that constrains such speech, and to be public and political in a world that diminishes both. It is worth noting that the community each has built is a women's community in terms of who is present as well as who is served. It is a community dominated by mothers and women care givers. Men are not totally absent from the preschool community, but they are often peripheral or marginal to the daily life and the central concerns.

Chana describes her networks and political projects as tied intimately to her child-care center. Her caring for children is what forces her into the political world, and her political work is what allows her to continue her work with children. For JoAnne, Anna, and Maya, working to enable children to grow and to learn also makes them powerful in the world, and these two aspects of empowerment are inseparable. JoAnne describes her friendships and her projects outside of day care as emanating from her work and linked directly to it. And Darlene, Maya, and Michele, while each names a variety of roles she plays in the world—from mother and sister to wife and friend—see themselves most productive and integrated as teachers. Each sees the identities and responsibilities as enriching each other, and sees herself centrally as a teacher.

There are, of course, teachers who are narrower in their concerns and more clearly bounded in their jobs than these outstanding teachers are. And yet, teaching is the kind of activity that calls out strongly for an investing of oneself. For many, perhaps most, teachers, the sense of calling exists. It may be only a flicker of memory or a feeling dulled by years of bureaucratic maneuvering, endless demands, and excruciating complexity; it may exist now only as a shadowy palimpsest, that little erasure that leaves tracks on the page. But somewhere along the way, teaching called out to teachers as a chance to love children, to make a difference in their lives, to remake the world. Teachers somewhere, sometime felt called to teach.

It is possible that the kind of intense observations and autobiographical work described here has created the illusion of teaching as identity by distorting the dailiness of teaching and reifying only a few moments. Yet the work may help to reveal and even make this integration accessible, and the synthesis would not be possible if the coherent elements did not already exist (see Appendix B).

It is likely that teaching as identity is intensified for these teachers because each is an outstanding practitioner. It is also possible that it is intensified for them as preschool teachers, who as a group are devalued in society. For each, teaching preschool is a choice that involves encountering a struggle for existence. The struggle is concrete—money and insurance, space and legal requirements—and more abstract—dignity and self-esteem and status. In either case, there are survival issues that require a marshaling of resources and strengths, and a projection of oneself into the world. Because preschool teaching is only a vague and amorphous profession-in-formation, these teachers are less likely to look at themselves through some predetermined and dominant lens, the way other teachers, almost in spite of themselves, increasingly look through the trade union lens. Preschool teachers are in this sense both more oppressed and less constrained than others.

## SOCIAL SCIENCE AND TEACHER PORTRAITS

These portraits are self-made and subjective. They are the result of ethnographic inquiry and autobiographical reflection. There is a feeling of the personal, the specific, and the unique about them. And yet there is also something familiar about them, something common and something shared. Looking at these portraits with an eye to what social scientists have told us about teaching amplifies some familiar themes.

Chana writes about having "too many challenges for the hours in a day—every day," and one remembers Philip Jackson's (1968) description of teachers experiencing the attack of time and the "here and now urgency" of their work (p. 119). Jackson speculated that teachers have about 1000 interpersonal interactions every day, and this figure may be considerably higher for these teachers of young children with their more intense needs and their extended day.

Teachers, Jackson found, are bound by immediacy, spontaneity, excitement, and variety. Teachers, like actors on a stage, rely on "fleeting behavioral cues" (p. 119) from their audiences in order to adjust and move on. Teachers, when asked by Jackson to discuss their own teaching successes, never referred to objective evidence of student progress. Rather, teachers overwhelmingly referred to the present moment, to a time when they stimulated a student's enthusiasm, involvement, and interest.

Jackson's sense that teachers rely heavily on spontaneity and on the value of the moment echoes Dan Lortie's (1975) finding that teachers are oriented to a kind of "presentism." When Michele describes the reward of teaching, she refers to the power of a moment, to the intense looks on the faces of children, to the sense of satisfaction when a problem is solved. Maya refers to no so-called objective evidence to defend her assessment of success; she simply points to the moment in all its color and its glory. Darlene describes the reward of teaching as being "right there when it happens," when a child learns something new. Similarly, JoAnne elevates spontaneity to a principle, when she argues against planning that might interfere with the excitement and value of each encounter.

Informality for Jackson involves a sense of spontaneity, engagement, and preferred teaching style. It is linked to autonomy in the sense that what teachers fear most is inflexible curricula and administrative interference that sufficiently undermines both professional judgment and spontaneity, the informal core of learning. Michele jokes about "powerful forces" cutting down her available space and constraining her teaching. She complains of "numbers and money," too many kids and too few resources, as the central problems of teaching. Chana criticizes parents, in a sense an outside force comparable to the administration in her situation, for not understanding the program, for imposing selfish needs onto her and the children, for pushing in directions that will limit her autonomy. And Darlene worries that too many people, especially the government, just don't care.

Jackson focuses on individuality, especially teachers' persistent interest in individual students. Satisfaction in teaching is attained through success with a particular student. When JoAnne described the reward of teaching, she named several individual children and then launched into a story about one of her favorites. Similarly, Michele describes no cool job satisfaction, but rather says she gets "goosebumps" when a difficult child responds.

In discussing teacher satisfaction, Jackson prefers the word "joy," a more accurate term, he contends, for the committed professionals of his study. While "satisfaction" adequately describes the sense of being useful, serving a worthy cause, and accomplishing good work, "joy" is a better word for the sense of excitement about the unexpected breakthroughs in teaching, the exhilaration and "thrill of witnessing dramatic change" (p. 138), and the wholehearted investments we see in outstanding teachers. Darlene says that all moments are special for young children, and the passion of teaching is the "here and now intimacy" of growth.

Donald Schön (1983) describes practitioners like teachers engaging in reflective conversation with unique situations. "Reflective practitioners" are those interactive professionals whose work is based less on science or a model of technical rationality and more on this reflective conversation. The reflective conversation has its roots in a practical knowledge not easily accessible to outsiders, nor easily codified and technicized. Schön identifies as strengths some of the very qualities many researchers bemoan as personal weaknesses. The difference is one of history and context: For some, teachers exercise a feminine birthright in their intuitive and tender ways, and those people wish teachers could overcome these traits on the road to becoming more professional. Schön recasts the intuitive as a legitimate, though undervalued, form of knowing, and he resists the notion of forcing professional knowledge into a prescribed technical vocabulary. When we listen to Chana describing her thinking as she works to help first one and then another child and mother to separate successfully, we gain insight into what Schön has in mind. Michele's struggle to reach out and teach the child with Down's Syndrome is another concrete example of reflective practice.

Jackson refers to the paradox of "present-oriented teachers in future-oriented-institutions" (1968, p. 126). This may appear more of a paradox than it is in fact. There may also be a certain logical consistency in teachers giving the teaching moment its due. Teachers, after all, live the teaching moment with their children, and in living it fully they acknowledge the obvious: that life in school is life nonetheless. JoAnne, for example, discusses the importance of respecting and empowering young children for the value it has at the moment and because that moment will remain a part of the life of those children. Each teacher discusses her work in terms of caring at the moment, of compassion, of connection. These traditionally female themes, often denigrated or dismissed, are elevated in the work of Nel Noddings (1984) and others as legitimate and essential ways of thinking about teaching. Noddings develops a notion of caring as fundamental to teaching and criticizes attempts to subordinate relatedness and receptivity to reason. She argues that caring and compassion must be elevated as they are understood in a different epistemological framework.

Dan Lortie (1975) talks about the low status of teachers and the many problems that that creates for the profession. One problem is a kind of denial of self, a discourse that is "self-accusing rather than self-accepting" (p. 159). Each of the teachers in this study is articulate and precise in her condemnation of the low status of teaching and is acutely aware of the ways preschool teaching is further devalued and of the even further gradations and degradations of day care and family day care. And yet, ironically, each has also internalized aspects of the lowly status and each participates in subtle ways in a kind of self-condemnation. For example, I discovered that each was surprised that someone wanted to study her, and in the beginning a common concern that the teachers had was they would have nothing to contribute.

A related problem, according to Lortie, is the low occupational commitment of teachers, the "in and out" nature of the job. Lortie claims that 60 percent of the married women teachers he studied said they would leave teaching after having a child. Changes in their husbands' careers or life situations were also cited as reasons these women would leave teaching. Further, 58 percent of the beginning women teachers in Lortie's study said they planned to return to the classroom after they raised their children. All of this, according to Lortie, indicates the tentative nature of women's occupational commitment.

I would be hard-pressed to describe the occupational commitments of these preschool teachers as low or tentative, even though each has had an in-and-out affair with teaching. These teachers, rather, are fierce in the face of overwhelming odds—persistent against inadequate pay, low or nonexistent benefits, legal constraints, and constant pressure. Each more clearly reflects "perseverance in the face of obstacles" (Laws, 1976, p. 36). Whereas Lortie takes the fact that 58 percent of women teachers plan to interrupt their careers as *prima facie* evidence of low commitment, Laws considers the fact that the same 58 percent plan to return to the classroom as a demonstration of incredible tenacity, given the life situation of women.

Several critics argue that we must turn our models of career upside down, taking into account women's experiences. Clearly, women who shoulder childbearing, child-rearing, and household responsibilities as well as career commitments would compare favorably with men whose situation is "conducive to occupational attainment" (Laws, 1976, p. 36). Women might well be viewed as the more committed, since they must contend with a variety of barriers in their pursuit of career, even as they continue to perform the unwaged labor of home and family; while men traditionally pursue a career with the invisible aid and support of un-waged workers in the home. The organization of work in our society assumes a male supremacist model, a model of breadwinning men and un-waged women domestic workers whose production and reproduction are dependent on those men. Rather than accept this situation as a given, as a natural state of affairs that constitutes the taken-for-granted background to inquiry and understanding, critics argue that male supremacy has historical roots and structures that must be perceived in order to understand the true situation of women's work.

Michael Apple (1985) describes the historical division of labor along gender lines, delineating both a vertical division where women receive lower pay and have worse working conditions than their male counterparts, and a horizontal division where women are concentrated in the lowest-paying and lowest-status jobs. The low status of teaching is in part a result of the fact that it is women's work, which is systematically devalued in our society. As teaching became women's work, a process of hierarchical control, supervision, and "de-skilling" began that continues to this day. This de-skilling involves the persistent drive for outside control by administrators, state bureaucrats, curriculum specialists, and academics, all male-dominated professions. Teaching, the work of women, is constrained and circumscribed by certification requirements, policy directives, teacher competencies, and curriculum mandates, all the work of men.

Anna, JoAnne, Darlene, Michele, Maya, and Chana are teachers who exemplify much of what has been written about teachers by social scientists: the sense of urgency, of practicality, of present-orientation, of seeking primary rewards from children. And yet each also demonstrates what it means to be grounded in a posture of caring and concern, and to carry on this most demanding, devalued, and complex enterprise with grace and creativity.

## TOWARD AN AUTOBIOGRAPHICAL METHOD

There is, of course, more to say. The work reported on here is incomplete. It offers no definitive or final statement, and it could be further enriched by the inclusion of dozens of other portraits. This work is one piece of the long-range project of understanding teaching and teachers.

Robert Bellah and co-authors (1985) noted that "finding oneself means, among other things, finding the story or narrative in terms of which one's life makes sense" (p. 81). For Anna, Darlene, Maya, JoAnne, Michele, and Chana, working out autobiographical accounts was in part a process of making sense and self-discovery. These teacher-autobiographies provide the kind of detail from which one can interpret practice, value, and belief in light of an unfolding story. For teacher educators, researchers, and especially teachers themselves who are seeking understanding and meaning in their work, this enterprise may provide a means of stretching their own contexts. Dan Lortie (1975) advocated using student-autobiographies as well as literature and biography in teacher education as a way "to increase the person's awareness of his [sic] beliefs and preferences about teaching and to have him expose them to personal examination" (p. 231). This would allow a teacher to "become truly selective and work out a synthesis of past and current practices in terms of his own values and understandings" (p. 231).

Lortie also compares teaching unfavorably with other human service work in this respect:

> Social workers, clinical psychologists, and psychotherapists are routinely educated to consider their own personalities and to take them into account in their work with people. Their stance is supposed to be analytic and open; one concedes and works with one's own limitations—it is hoped—in a context of self-acceptance. The tone of teacher interviews and their rhetoric reveals no such orientation; I would characterize it as moralistic rather than analytic and self-accusing rather than self-accepting. (p. 159)

Rob Traver (1987) advocates an autobiographical method of research on teaching, a method that emphasizes "the first person perspective of the teacher, a perspective that includes the intellectual, ethical, and emotional stance of the teacher while he or she is engaged in and reflecting on teaching" (p. 443). First person accounts move the teacher into dialogue with other teachers and lead to "a new consciousness about the intelligence, ethics, and emotions of teaching," a consciousness that does "not contain the silence of the old one" (p. 444).

This new consciousness is a beginning, but it is not enough. William Pinar (1986) describes autobiography as a "returning home," conscious of origins and better able to integrate issues from the past into the present. But, he asks:

> Once home, is the issue resolved? The issue of authenticity may be, but the educational issue remains. What did I make of what I have been made? . . . As significant as self-knowledge and authenticity are, as important as it is now for teachers to exemplify as well as know these *modes d'être*, they do not constitute historical end states. They set the stage for asking: What attitudes and actions are appropriate given this self-knowledge? (p. 4)

It would seem possible that work organized around deeply held beliefs that are grounded in a strong political sense and experience and that result in certain core organizing principles upon which one is willing to act could move one's work from the ordinary to the excellent, from the mundane to the transcendental. A successful autobiographical method has positive implications for allowing greater questioning, critique, and intentionality.

The work described here moves in the direction of an autobiographical method for general use. It requires no special expertise or credentials or affiliations. Rather, this method of teacher self-awareness and self-report is suited to teachers' study groups as well as teacher education seminars, to informal teacher networks as well as more organized school improvement efforts. What is essential is a desire and a willingness on the part of teachers themselves to engage in this effort. It demands concentration and activity on the part of teachers; it assumes that teachers can grow and change and choose and learn; and it assumes that teaching and learning are only possibilities that require intention, desire, and assertion to become realities.

This method seeks meaning in reflection and metaphor as well as in action and behavior. It involves classroom observations of teachers teaching, and pedagogical dialogues of teachers reflecting on their lives as they influence teaching practices. It demands collaboration on the part of teacher and observer toward the production of a meaningful narrative text that describes and links together influences, events, people, and experiences that contribute to the creation of the teacher as she finds herself today. This text, assumed to be neither comprehensive nor complete, becomes the focus for the teacher to critically examine her teaching practices and to locate them in a continuum from past to future.

While there does not need to be any set format for the different accounts, it might be useful to remember the three broad areas of inquiry discussed in Chapter 1. These areas are the reflective practitioner, in which practice is probed and critically examined; the autobiographer, in which an account is created of one's life; and the whole person, in which activity outside teaching is discussed and brought into focus. What is significant is the developing story and anything that allows the story to become richer, deeper, and more vivid in a meaningful way. "Reconstructed logic" (Kaplan, 1963), the purely formal and consistent recasting of knowledge, is less useful here than "logic-in-use," which covers intuition and insight, discovery and invention. Every effort must be made to search deeply enough so that the story moves beyond the taken-for-granted, the expected response, and the social science jargon, which has become in our modern world the dominant way in which we experience and make sense of ourselves. The point is not to achieve a sanitized, objective truth, but rather an expanded sense of understanding of a subject. Perhaps accuracy is not the goal at all, but rather access to the myths that tell what teaching is like for teachers. The search is for whatever events are salient, whatever moments dramatic, whatever changes remarkable. The quest is for epiphany (what James Joyce called "insight into the whatness of the thing") and the mundane, for surprise and penetration, and for significant patterns discovered through textual analysis and comparison. When the story fails to generate new insight, when it merely recapitulates existing data, when "theoretical saturation" (Glaser & Strauss, 1967), more commonly known as boredom, is reached, then the story is done for the moment.

Observations can be formal and planned, or informal. They can be sustained or fleeting. Self-observation, journal-writing, and the like can contribute to the work. Interviews and conversations are a part of creating a narrative text, and so are interpretive activities, as described in Chapter 1. Interpretive activities might include mapping one's pathway to teaching using a variety of collage materials, or depicting a successful moment in teaching using clay, or creating an image of learning something using colored paper and paint.

In studying teachers holistically, we will also begin to understand teaching and learning more fully. In talking with teachers we will enrich our collective understanding of children. In recent years several of the commonsense assumptions about children (for example, the assumption that young children engage in parallel play and are incapable of deep social interactions) have been challenged by teachers themselves. Amplifying the voice of teachers will accelerate our insights into childhood and could lead to a more phenomenological direction in early childhood education. In listening to teachers more fully, we are also afforded the opportunity of seeing children more completely.

This, of course, raises the question of why teachers and researchers are distinct professionals in the field of education, and whether there could be value in evolving toward a concept of teacher-researchers. Rob Traver (1987) pushes in this direction:

> To the extent that we believe that understanding people requires first that they speak with their own words, we must admit that we know very little. We must, therefore, think about ways that make it possible to listen to teachers, to respect their intelligence, ethic, and emotion, to ask them to keep journals and memoirs, to share classes and meals, and to help them write and speak. What this means is that we must seek teacher empowerment within the academic culture of the study of teaching. (p. 446)

Eleanor Duckworth (1986) takes the point further, arguing that teachers, like psychiatrists and practitioners in other fields, are in the best position to conduct research on teaching because of their intimate engagement with the material researched. She argues that "teaching, practiced as a process of engaging learners in trying to make sense, might be the sine qua non of such research" (p. 494) and asks, "Why should this be a separate research profession?" (p. 495). She concludes, "There is no reason I can think of not to rearrange the resources available for education so that this description defines the job of a public school teacher" (p. 495).

Early childhood education as a separate field is experiencing enormous growth now, accompanied by predictable uncertainty about identity and direction. There are many important questions still unsettled: What defines the field of early childhood education? In what ways is it a profession? What are the contradictions within the field and the likely directions of resolution? Who are the people in the field? How do they see themselves? It is not a fully articulated profession, but is rather a patchwork of disparate bits and pieces. As early childhood educators move toward self-definition in a period of flux, it will be important to move beyond the perspective of managers and policy makers and to understand the perspective of the practitioners themselves.

Since a profession is a group that self-consciously declares its beliefs and opinions, it will be critical to know what it is that early childhood people profess. Is it a group that advocates for the young child? How? Is it a group that develops partnerships with parents and families? In what ways? What is the proper place of professional preparation in the development of early childhood teachers?

There are political issues in the formation of a profession as well. How do early childhood educators talk about resources and their distribution, for example? What is the educators' relationship to the school system and its traditional role in reproducing the existing social relations? Do they enhance or substitute for the family? Is there any relationship between their work and a more just social order?

Early childhood education is a field of possibilities. Asking these kinds of questions, seeking answers from the practitioners themselves, and creating dialogue among teachers, parents, children, and others could prove to be exciting and critical to the future of the profession and of all children.

## THE GOOD PRESCHOOL TEACHER

Who, then, is the good preschool teacher? We have seen here six examples of fine preschool teachers and have discussed some of the patterns that emerge from the portraits of these six. Is that all there is? Are there any prescriptions to be drawn from these examples? Are there other possible ways to be good?

Certainly these teachers highlight for us qualities that we would look for in good teachers, qualities like a commitment to dialogue and to interaction with children; an attitude of relatedness and receptivity, concern and compassion for the ways and lives of children; an active investment in and passion for the world, or a piece of it, and for meaningful knowledge and information that allow human beings to function fully and freely. This is heavy and quite general, and yet it only begins to answer our question, for dialogue, compassion, and love of knowledge have different meanings in different contexts. Dialogue, for example, does not exist outside of people, and people exist in different stages of growth, multiple historical and social contexts, and endless variety. Dialogue may be principle, but it is not prescription. Compassion may be foundation, but it is not formula.

Teaching is often discussed as discrete behaviors or universal practices. Teaching is often dissected, counted, and subjected to detailed analysis. While some of this effort brings knowledge and insight, much of it does violence to something fundamental in teaching, that is, that teaching cannot exist outside of a person, and people cannot exist outside of situations. While computers can do many things teachers do, for the computer the doing has no deeper significance. It is not simply that computers do what human intelligence and interest tell them to do; it is that computers lack intention. Teachers have intentions, desires, motives, and goals. Teachers exist and make choices in contexts. Teaching requires a subject. Understanding teaching, then, demands relationships with people, and that invites an openness to feelings, ideals, aspirations, failures, successes, and more.

Of course, all of us who labor in an uncertain and imperfect world would welcome an answer with a capital "A." And yet, somewhere we must also realize that there are no answers that settle everything and that if there were, that would reduce human life immeasurably. To be human is to project forward, to create new possibilities, to imagine the world as if it could be otherwise. This means, among other things, that the past, too, is changing, is something to be transcended and reinterpreted.

Teaching is an achievement, not an endowment. Teaching is created in an intersubjective reality, in webs of relationships, in community. Because teachers are the instruments of their own teaching, they are thrust back on themselves as inventors of their own developing practice.

Schools, of course, are not neutral, and teaching is never value-free. Though it is sometimes difficult to discern in our own familiar contexts, it is plain when we look outside ourselves that schools are institutions embedded in given societies and that teaching is therefore problematic. If education is thought of as preparation for life in a society or as the effort of a community to reproduce and replenish itself, then we need to be able to recommend that society and warrant that community in some way. Justifying our teaching and our schools is plainly insufficient. We must somehow understand our multiple contexts as well. We must take responsibility for our connections and affiliations, even those that are not of our own choosing and making. It is not simply that schools are porous institutions, and that historical, economic, political, social, and cultural aspects touch school life fairly freely; it is, rather, that those dimensions become the essential ground for education.

And so we return to the good preschool teacher. We see a person who chooses and creates her teaching in a world not of her own choosing. We see a person who lives and works with ambiguity—who engages the questions in a world of uncertainty. And we see a kaleidoscope of possibility, for there are endless good preschool teachers, each grounded in a real situation, a living context; each caring, dreaming of a world where people care more, and working to make that more-caring world come to be.

# PARTING GLANCES
# All I Ever Really Needed to Know I Learned in Kindergarten

Most of what I really need to know about how to live, and what to do, and how to be, I learned in kindergarten. Wisdom was not at the top of the graduate school mountain but there in the sandbox at nursery school.

These are the things I learned: Share everything. Play fair. Don't hit people. Put things back where you found them. Clean up your own mess. Don't take things that aren't yours. Say you're sorry when you hurt somebody. Wash your hands before you eat. Flush. Warm cookies and cold milk are good for you. Live a balanced life. Learn some and think some and draw and paint and sing and dance and play and work every day some.

Take a nap every afternoon. When you go out into the world, watch for traffic, hold hands and stick together. Be aware of wonder. Remember the little seed in the plastic cup. The roots go down and the plant goes up and nobody really knows how or why, but we are all like that. Goldfish and hamsters and white mice and even the little seed in the plastic cup— they all die. So do we.

And then remember the book about Dick and Jane and the first word you learned, the biggest word of all: LOOK. Everything you need to know is in there somewhere. The Golden Rule and love and basic sanitation. Ecology and politics and sane living.

Think of what a better world it would be if we all—the whole world— had cookies and milk about three o'clock every afternoon and then lay down with our blankets for a nap. Or if we had a basic policy in our nation and other nations to always put things back where we found them and cleaned up our own messes. And it is still true, no matter how old you are, when you go out into the world, it is best to hold hands and stick together.

ROBERT FULGHUM

# APPENDIX A
# A Particular Autobiography

As noted earlier, since the researcher is the explicit instrument of this kind of inquiry, rigor demands clarification of position, ground, and context. At every point along the way in this study, I was making choices that would ultimately affect the final product of this project—which teachers to observe, where to focus my gaze, and what material to select. Thus, it is reasonable to ask for a personal accounting that will allow an independent judgment concerning the validity of this work. Since this study is rooted in autobiography, it is fair to ask for my own autobiographical account. What are my background and training? Where did I come from and how did I get here? What is my theoretical orientation? What are my personal values and feelings? What are my goals? There is no doubt that, as is true of any research of any type, my attitudes, values, and goals had a substantial effect on the process of this work as well as on the final report; the reader deserves to know, therefore, my orientation and my relationship to the teachers involved, in order to assess and understand the value of what has been found here. Of course, my narrative, like the others, is brief, selective, and subjective. Because this is not a road map, it may be confounding to some, but it is offered as an impression of a life, which may help to ground the reading of other lives.

To begin, I was born in the Midwest, at the tail end of the Second World War. I grew up in privilege and in the surface calm of the 1940s and 1950s. Of course, underneath, the world was churning, boiling, and changing rapidly and irrevocably. I remember vaguely gasoline rationing and squeezing the margarine bag to distribute the little red color dot (now known to be carcinogenic) throughout the fat. I remember vividly the black "cleaning lady" who in her silence bespoke a world beyond my neat suburban nest, and I remember the first television set down the block, and a year or so later, our own. I remember going from coal to oil heat, and I remember the first frozen foods, the first McDonald's, and all the early electric household gadgets. I remember men returning from war, and I can still see in my mind the body of the teenager across the street being carried from his home by medics after he blew his brains out with a handgun.

My clearest memory is of my large, caring family, from whom I learned something of what Barbara Biber described as "the taste and the boundary of freedom, the comfort and irritation of being controlled, the safety and threat of being known." I am the middle child of five, and that fact continues to shade relationships and interactions. Cathy is always the oldest, the solid one. Tim is my big brother, even though we've shared adult lives for almost 25 years. Rick is my little brother, though taller, and John is the baby, the object of everyone's affection—of course—and hence the magnet, the center, the peacemaker. As a middle child, I had occasion to learn and to teach; I had a couple of strong role models, and I modeled for others. I feel reverberations, stirrings of memory, when I watch my own middle child look with awe and admiration at everything his older brother can do, even the silly and the destructive things, or when I watch him deftly and agreeably play up to his older brother's expectations and then down to his younger brother's. The intensity of that early awakening to social relationships fades but is never really erased.

I liked school. I liked the social life and the sports, but I also liked academics, and I worked hard, if erratically, in school. The teachers I remember best are the ones who treated me on some level with care. While I can't remember a single equation from algebra, for example, I remember Mr. Ainsworth as a caring and wonderful teacher. He reached out to me as a person. My family set high standards, and Cathy and Tim modeled certain behavior: reading widely and avidly, for example, being on time and prepared—things that are automatic with me still. Cathy personified a sense of intellectual excellence, winning all the academic prizes, and Tim a sense of talent and personality, being elected class president one year and "most popular boy" another.

Our parents expected us to succeed in school, but their values included a sense of individual development. They were "Dr. Spock parents," a fact that undoubtedly causes some confusion and discomfort for them now, given Dr. Spock's current political projects, but the label was something that fit them at the time. From preschool through high school, I remember my parents as well-liked by other kids, who felt a sense of caring and respect from them. While I had a clear sense of high standards, I didn't feel either the striving and pushing that sometimes accompany that goal, or the insistence on a single prescribed path. Rather, I was encouraged to find my own way in an atmosphere of warmth and support.

I read Jack Kerouac's (1955) book *On the Road* when I was thirteen, and reread it several times over the next six years. Kerouac captured a youthful excitement about life, a feeling of being special, and a yearning for a way out of life's straitjackets and constrained expectations. He wrote of a world of shattered ideals and the wreckage and the hypocrisy on the moral landscape that resonated for me and for many in the post-war generation. I, too, felt that "the only people for me are the mad ones, the ones who are mad to live, mad to talk, mad to be saved, desirous of everything at the same time, the ones who never yawn or say a commonplace thing, but burn, burn, burn like fabulous yellow roman candles exploding like spiders across the stars" (p. 9). I shared their "ragged and ecstatic joy of pure being" (p. 161) and spent time in coffeehouses and parks and lofts listening to poets and singers, philosophers, improvisers, musicians, and hipsters.

I went to the University of Michigan in 1963, where the aching to live and find meaning in life became focused and refined. In 1962, a group centered at the University had written a manifesto called the Port Huron Statement. It began: "We are people of this generation, bred in at least modest comfort, housed now in universities, looking uncomfortably to the world we inherit." I joined Students for a Democratic Society (SDS), who I felt were the most thoughtful, caring, hopeful, and daring group of people I had ever known. I was involved in civil rights demonstrations and struggles, reflections of the mighty drama being played primarily in the South but with moral ramifications across the land. When the war in Vietnam escalated, calling out protest and opposition, I felt a natural link between these two causes. Along with others of my generation, I thought that working collectively we had the intellectual power to inquire into and understand the world, and acting together we had the passion and commitment to remake it. I felt that we could be both dreamers and doers. I believed strongly in the need for people to act on behalf of their values and their ideals, and I organized around that basic belief. To this day I admire people who are willing to take risks for their beliefs, and I am disappointed in those who see themselves only as victims, unable to choose, and not responsible for outcomes.

I began to teach in 1965 in an experimental free school in Ann Arbor called the Children's Community. The Children's Community was founded by three mothers who had been part of the civil rights and political movements and were influenced in their thinking about education by the writings of A. S. Neill, Sylvia Ashton-Warner, Paul Goodman, and John Holt. These three mothers felt uneasy about sending their own children into schools they perceived as racist, competitive, and destructive of learning and growth, and so they started their own school. Becoming a teacher was, for me, a natural part of an ongoing commitment to the ideal of freedom and justice. Teaching was, in part, an expression of my desire to do socially productive work, to make a positive difference in people's lives, to help create a more just social order. There were values and passions important to me that I could experience and express, hold and share in my work with youngsters. I also came to teaching because I loved children, or being with children; or perhaps more accurately, I loved the way I was when I was with children. Teaching called out the best in me, I thought, and was a way for me to be in the world that felt right and good. I look back today on my experiences with Michael, Renée, Scot, Duke, Kevin, Tony, Cory, Margie, Darlene, Mona, Annie, Timineet, Mwaniki, Isadora, Sasi, Max, Christy, Lynette, Salome, Britt, and many others, and I know that the quality of my life is better for having worked with them. I believe their lives are better for it, too, and that we are traveling on. These things remain for me the reasons to teach.

In 1965 I was arrested for a sit-in at the Ann Arbor draft board. Over the next few years I was arrested several times for acting in opposition to the Vietnam War and to racism, including two arrests during the demonstrations at the Democratic National Convention in Chicago in 1968. There was at that time a growing sense in me, and among many other young people, of the need for militancy and internationalism, and of the importance of creating a community of resistance to what we deemed unacceptable. I believed that only by our taking further personal risk on behalf of our beliefs and our goals, by deepening and broadening our resistance, was the movement to end the war and create a more peaceful, more just, and more democratic and humane society likely to succeed. I left teaching in 1969 and for the next several years worked as a teamster, a laborer, a stevedore, a baker, and a farm worker, but my energy and heart were invested in organizing and acting against the war.

When the war ended, I and the woman I had lived and worked with all those years had our first child. My energy turned back toward children, and my ongoing desire to work with children and to create a more caring world in that context took on a deeper, more personal meaning for me. Zayd became the organizing center of our lives. I began to teach again in 1978, this time in day care. In 1980 Malik was born, and in 1981 we adopted Chesa. As every parent can understand, these three transformed our lives and brought us more intense joy, humor, tragedy, and pain than we had ever known. And it is from this vantage point that I now look at teaching.

I met JoAnne in 1978 when she was first organizing a day-care center and we enrolled Zayd in her program. She was caregiver to all three of our children over the years, and she and I were colleagues and co-workers for seven years. I learned a lot from JoAnne about working with young children, and our relationship became a close personal and professional one.

That same year JoAnne and I hired Darlene, who has been a friend ever since. We have been colleagues to one another and teachers of one another's children.

I met Anna in 1980 through a friend who told me she was an extraordinary teacher I ought to observe. I visited her classroom on several occasions simply to get ideas for my own teaching. Later we became friends.

In 1983 I met Michele when she enrolled two of her children in our program. I was a teacher of her children for two years, and then in 1985 Malik was a student in her public school kindergarten class, so we have had a unique parent-teacher, teacher-parent relationship.

I met Maya in 1983 at a conference on early childhood education. She led an engaging workshop on reading with young children, and I introduced myself to her and asked if I could visit her classroom. She agreed, and I visited her several times over the next few years.

I met Chana through JoAnne in 1986 when I was searching for a family day-care provider for this project. Coincidentally, our children attended the same school that year.

Making sense of all that I have seen and heard through these teachers clearly goes beyond the particular words and incidents, and resonates with my own experience as a day-care worker, early childhood teacher, student, teacher educator, son, and father. The story I have told, then, is indeed a story of six teachers, but it is also my own story.

# APPENDIX B
## Disturbance in the Field

As this project unfolded, I began to wonder how my presence was affecting these teachers. Was I stirring things up in either a positive or a negative way? Were they pleased or displeased with the process of the work? And how was the project affecting me? I remembered Michele's comment when she looked at a draft of her own portrait: "There are things I like about it. I like being seen in such a positive light. But there's also something unreal. I'm not that good, and you know it. You never show me when I've lost it and am going up the walls." And then, almost as an afterthought, she jokingly said, "Maybe I'm on my best behavior when I see you coming through that door." This could be important. How did the others experience my comings and goings? In what ways was I a disturbance in the field?

I had thought that these teachers primarily felt energized by this project, that the consistent attention and opportunity to discuss their work outside of the context of their individual settings created a sense of being valued and honored. There was, of course, a smaller subtheme of people feeling nervous in my presence, as if my looking deeply might reveal aspects that were not for public scrutiny. Michele's sense of there being "something unreal" in my account of her work is an example of this. I wondered if this feeling was universal, and further if it was tied to the way status and power are divided in our society between researcher and practitioner and between men and women. I decided to organize a meeting to discuss these issues, thinking that a group meeting might provide a sense of strength and solidarity for these teachers. Chana, Michele, Darlene, and I met for dinner at JoAnne's apartment and talked for several hours about these and other issues.

The clearest theme to emerge from this meeting was that of being honored and energized by the research project. JoAnne described each interview as leaving her feeling "energized and restless." She wrote a vignette in which she described feeling "flattered" to be a subject in a study. "Somehow this validates my work," she said, "and provides me with more confidence that I am a good teacher and that I have something to offer others." JoAnne felt that the close scrutiny of her work and the extensive interviewing and interest in her ideas helped her to focus on her work and recommit herself to it at a time when "I've been distracted because of the intensity of the adoption process."

JoAnne added that she liked "seeing patterns, like my thriving on responsibility or wanting to be of use, fall into place." She claims that these patterns were things that she had always known about herself but that they remained unstated and inaccessible to her for the most part. Once revealed, they were instantly familiar and things that she could now employ consciously and productively. So this disturbance in JoAnne's field is an example of how the project contributed to a fuller sense of self-formation and self-declaration.

For JoAnne there was also a concrete practical result to the work: "My mind was racing all night after the first interview, and I felt much clearer about what I was doing at work and what my goals for children were. I got up and wrote out a curriculum guide, which we're working on as an addition to our parent handbook. We've also begun to develop activities like using clay to create an image of your teaching in our staff development." JoAnne liked the image she created of her teaching, a figure reading a book with two smaller figures on her lap. She plans to save the clay figure to give her strength on the "bad days."

Darlene felt that talking about the work was "like therapy," and Michele had a similar reaction. "I felt honored," she said. "I felt that you were different from other observers because I knew you knew what to look for. When you saw the things I wanted seen, and then wrote them down and made them sound so fine, that was lovely." Michele also described the difficult experience with Ashley as having been affected by this research. "It helped me to know that you were watching. Somehow it made me want it to work more."

Chana concurred. "I miss being a student," she said. "That was an outlet, a time to think about what I was doing, a focus. This has some of that about it. It legitimizes what I do, and it's a space where I don't have to generate everything." Chana described how, on a day-to-day basis, the house can simply close in upon itself. "You bring in a different energy," she said. "You come because of the work, you come to honor the work. That's recognition and that's validation. That's important." Chana's point was not unequivocal: "Sometimes I want to tell you that the work speaks for itself, that I'm just a simple care giver. Your persistent questions don't allow that—they make it more complex, inexplicable almost, hard to talk about."

For Chana there was practical application too. "Just talking about Helen and Jimmy made me stronger," she said. "She came and wanted to drop him even though he had an ear infection, and I told her he was going to have too hard a time and he'd do better if she took him to her appointment. I wouldn't have said that if we hadn't been talking."

Chana is characteristically the first to raise a criticism of the work. "It's an intrusion mainly in terms of time. These questions are so provocative I could lose a whole day on them, and I don't have five minutes. I have so much to do, and this is another meeting." In an odd way I feel that way too. Occasionally when one of the teachers would have to cancel a meeting or an interview, I would be relieved. The tightness and the pressure of time is my main preoccupation also, and yet to be released from responsibility provided a momentary relief. There was relief too from the gnawing sense of guilt that I was imposing too much. The problem reasserted itself quickly, however, as I struggled against time to know more and to do more. No one else mentioned the problem of time, but it is a theme nonetheless, because of the difficulty each person had in scheduling meetings and setting up visits.

Michele raised the issue of my presence creating a sense of nervousness and anxiety. "I got over it eventually," she said, "but in the beginning I was feeling revealed and invaded." She attributed this feeling to the knowledge that the project would go beyond superficial observations: "You wanted to know who I am as a person." Her nervousness was justified in her own mind from an early reading of the work. "Some of what you saw was only vaguely familiar, and that unsettled me. To see unfamiliar things with my name in the center made me think I need to be more conscious. It made me more attentive." Chana, too, felt that she wanted the house to be perfect on those days scheduled for observation, and JoAnne inevitably felt after my visits that I had missed something magnificent that happened the day before or the day after I came. Each person had a sense of unreality or of hiding something or of fooling me, even though the dominant theme was one of validation and encouragement.

It would seem that the process of being involved in something like this has, in itself, the power to elevate one's teaching and call forth the best one has to offer. It is possible that a kind of steady empathetic scrutiny improves teaching. There is no reason whatsoever that this kind of work needs to be the exclusive province of university-based researchers. This method, it seems to me, could easily be adapted to action research projects, peer review, and teacher-run development projects.

# REFERENCES

Abbs, P. (1974). *Autobiography in education*. London: Heinemann Education Books.

Abbs, P. (1981). Education and the living image: Reflections on imagery, fantasy, and the art of recognition. *Teachers College Record, 82,* 475–496.

Agar, M. H. (1980). *The professional stranger: An informal introduction to ethnography.* New York: Academic Press.

Apple, M. W. (1985). Teaching and "women's work": A comparative historical and ideological analysis. *Teachers College Record, 86,* 3, 455–473.

Ashton-Warner, S. (1958). *Spinster.* New York: Touchstone.

Ashton-Warner, S. (1963). *Teacher.* New York: Touchstone.

Ashton-Warner, S. (1979). *I passed this way.* New York: Alfred A. Knopf.

Bateson, M. C. (1984). *With a daughter's eye.* New York: William Morrow and Co.

Beginnings. (1986). Meeting teachers: A newsletter for parents. *Beginnings: The magazine for teachers of young children, 3,* p. 25.

Bellah, R. N., Madsen, R., Sullivan, W. M., Swidler, A., and Tipton, S. M. (1985). *Habits of the heart.* New York: Harper & Row.

Berger, P. L. (1963). *Invitation to sociology.* Garden City, NY: Anchor Books.

Bolin, F. (1986). Vocational choice and the realities of teaching. Unpublished program outline for the Institute on Teaching, Teachers College, Columbia University, July 1986.

Denton, D. E. (1974). That mode of being called teaching. In David E. Denton, ed., *Existentialism and phenomenology in education* (99–115). New York: Teachers College Press.

Duckworth, E: (1986). Teaching as research. *Harvard Educational Review, 56,* 4, 481–495.

Eisner, E. W. (1977). On the uses of educational connoisseurship and criticism for evaluating classroom life. *Teachers College Record, 78,* 1–15.

Feiman-Nemser, S. and Floden, R. E. (1984). The cultures of teaching. East Lansing, MI: The Institute for Research on Teaching.

Geertz, C. (1973). *The interpretation of cultures.* New York: Basic Books.

Geertz, C. (1988). *Works and lives: The anthropologist as author.* Stanford: Stanford University Press.

Glaser, B. G. and Strauss, A. L. (1967). *The discovery of grounded theory: Strategies for qualitative research.* New York: Aldine Publishing Co.

Greene, M. (1978). *Landscapes of learning.* New York: Teachers College Press.

Grumet, M. (1978). Supervision and situation: A methodology of self-report for teacher education. *Journal of Curriculum Theorizing, 1,* 1, 191–257.

Jackson, P. W. (1968). *Life in classrooms.* New York: Holt, Rinehart and Winston.

Kaplan, A. (1963). *Conduct of inquiry: Methodology for behavioral science.* New York: Harper & Row.

Kerouac, J. (1955). *On the road.* New York: Viking Press.

Kohl, H. (1967). *36 Children.* New York: New American Library.

Laws, J. L. (1976). Work aspirations of women: False leads and new starts. *Signs: Journal of Women in Culture and Society, 1,* 3, 33–49.

Lightfoot, S. L. (1973). Politics and reasoning: Through the eyes of teachers and children. *Harvard Educational Review, 43,* 2, 197–244.

Lightfoot, S. L. (1983). *The good high school: Portraits of character and culture.* New York: Basic Books.

Lortie, D. C. (1975). *Schoolteacher: A sociological study.* Chicago: The University of Chicago Press.

Mandel, B. J. (1980). Full of life now. In James Olney, ed., *Autobiography: Essays theoretical and critical.* Princeton: Princeton University Press.

McDermott, R. P. (1977). Social relations as contexts for learning in school. *Harvard Educational Review, 47,* 2, 198–213.

Noddings, N. (1984). *Caring: A feminine approach to ethics and moral education.* Berkeley: University of California Press.

Overholt, G. E. and Stallings, W. M. (1976). Ethnographic and experimental hypotheses in educational research. *Educational Researcher, 5,* 12–14.

Pinar, W. F. (1975). Currere: Toward reconceptualization. In William F. Pinar, ed., *Curriculum theorizing.* Berkeley: McCutchan.

Pinar, W. F. (1986). Autobiography and the architecture of self. Louisiana State University. Unpublished paper.

Pratt, C. (1948). *I learn from children: An adventure in progressive education.* New York: Simon and Schuster.

Rutter, M., Maugham, B., Mortimer, P., and Ouston, J. (1979). *Fifteen thousand hours: Secondary schools and their effects on children.* Cambridge: Harvard University Press.

Sarason, S. B. (1982). *The culture of the school and the problem of change.* 2nd ed. Boston: Allyn and Bacon, Inc.

Sartre, J.-P. (1966). *Being and nothingness.* Translated by H. E. Barnes. New York: Washington Square Press.

Schön, D. A. (1983). *The reflective practitioner: How professionals think in action.* New York: Basic Books.

Schweder, R. A. (1988). The how of the word. *The New York Times Book Review,* February 28, 1988, p. 13.

Smith, L. and Keith, P. (1971). *Anatomy of an educational innovation.* New York: John Wiley and Sons, Inc.

Smyth, W. J. (1984). *Clinical supervision: Collaborative learning about teaching.* Australia: Deakin University Press.

Traver, R. (1987). Autobiography, feminism, and the study of teaching. *Teachers College Record, 88,* 3, 443–452.

Varenne, H. (1986). Ethnography in education. Unpublished course syllabus from Teachers College, Columbia University.

Wolcott, H. (n.d.). Study guide for ethnographic research methods in education. American Educational Research Association.

Yonemura, M. V. (1986). *A teacher at work: Professional development and the early childhood educator.* New York: Teachers College Press. Washington, DC.

# Index

# ABOUT THE AUTHOR

WILLIAM AYERS first taught preschool in 1965. He is currently Assistant Professor and Director of Elementary Education at the University of Illinois at Chicago. He earned his master's degree in early childhood education at the Bank Street College of Education, and his doctorate in curriculum and teaching at Teachers College, Columbia University. He is married and the father of three young children, whose growth and development spark and deepen his interest and investment in his work.